ADVANCE PRAISE

"This is a thoughtful reflection on the everyday choices that shape courageous leadership. A reminder that meaningful impact rarely comes from grand gestures alone but from consistent, values-driven action."
—PAUL POLMAN, BUSINESS LEADER, INVESTOR, PHILANTHROPIST

"Christopher Williams's book will help all of us master what is such a fundamental leadership attribute and cardinal virtue and simply be better, more effective leaders. Combining real-life stories, personal experiences, important concepts, and practical steps and tools, this book is a critical and urgent read in these challenging times."
—HUBERT JOLY, FORMER CHAIRMAN AND CEO OF BEST BUY, AUTHOR OF *THE HEART OF BUSINESS*

"C.O.U.R.A.G.E. reminds us that the key to transformation lies not in escaping fear but in embracing it with awareness and purpose. Christopher Williams offers a heartfelt and practical map for anyone ready to step beyond limitation and into the freedom of authentic living."
—DEEPAK CHOPRA, CONSCIOUSNESS EXPLORER AND *NEW YORK TIMES* BESTSELLING AUTHOR

"C.O.U.R.A.G.E. is a must-read for entrepreneurs, intrapreneurs, and anyone wrestling with the nagging feeling that something is missing despite outward success. Having worked closely with Christopher Williams, I have seen his outstanding leadership in action. Now he distills a lifetime of experience into a compelling guide for those seeking to make a real impact and live with purpose.

"This book is both a wake-up call and an opportunity for course correction—an invitation to step off autopilot and honestly assess whether the path you're on aligns with your authentic self. Chris masterfully articulates how courage is not the absence of fear but the consistent practice of making bold, values-driven choices. He offers a roadmap for those who sense they are meant for something more but need the clarity and confidence to take action.

"True transformation comes from daring to make the daily choices that shape a life of meaning, impact, and fulfillment. Chris challenges us to lean into courage—not just in big moments but in the small, intentional decisions that define who we become."

—FRED SWANIKER, FOUNDER AND CEO OF
SAND TECHNOLOGIES AND FOUNDER OF
AFRICAN LEADERSHIP GROUP

"Christopher Williams's C.O.U.R.A.G.E. taps into a single powerful idea—we all have the power to define and chase our own possibilities. Enjoy this read and ENJOY YOUR CHASE!"

—KEVIN CARROLL, AUTHOR, SPEAKER, CHANGE AGENT

C.O.U.R.A.G.E.

CHRISTOPHER O. H. WILLIAMS

C.O.U.R.A.G.E.

**7 CHOICES FOR LIVING
A LIFE WITHOUT REGRET**

COPYRIGHT © 2025 CHRISTOPHER O.H. WILLIAMS
All rights reserved.

C.O.U.R.A.G.E.
7 Choices for Living a Life Without Regret

FIRST EDITION

ISBN   978-1-5445-3309-4   *Hardcover*
            978-1-5445-3310-0   *Paperback*
            978-1-5445-3308-7   *Ebook*

To my inner circle:

My wife—my partner in life's unfolding journey, and two children—may your courage always lead you,

and, to

my late dad—for the gift of a compass, my mom—whose unwavering encouragement still lights my way, and my siblings—for your steadfast support and wise counsel. This book exists because of all you've enabled.

CONTENTS

FOREWORD 11
INTRODUCTION 13
1. THE HEART OF COURAGE 35
2. COMMIT TO A PURPOSE 57
3. OWN YOUR POTENTIAL 81
4. UNMASK FEAR 107
5. REJECT DISTRACTING VOICES 131
6. ACT DECISIVELY 161
7. GROW FROM FAILURE 191
8. EMBODY RESILIENCE (AND JOY) 213
CONCLUSION 239
IN GRATITUDE 247
ABOUT THE AUTHOR 253
REFERENCES 255

FOREWORD

—Helga Hengge, mountaineer, first German woman to successfully climb Mount Everest and the Seven Summits, and author of Only the Sky Above: My Journey to the Top of the World

When I climbed Mount Everest in 1999 and stood on the summit—the roof of the world—I understood something that had been true all along: Courage is not the absence of fear. Courage is taking the next step *despite* it.

The bitter cold, the thin air, the terrifying exposure—those are the obvious dangers. But the real obstacles were the quieter ones: the inner doubts, the judgment of others, the weight of expectation. These are the same forces many of us face in everyday life. You don't need to get lost in a storm or stand on a glacier in the midst of the Himalayas to encounter fear. You can meet it at your desk, in a boardroom, or alone with a life decision that scares you.

That's why *C.O.U.R.A.G.E.: 7 Choices for Living a Life Without Regret* by Christopher O. H. Williams resonated so deeply with me. This is not a book about performing extraordinary feats. It's about cultivating the one superpower that makes every worthy achievement possible: courage.

Christopher doesn't treat courage as something mystical or out of reach. Drawing from personal events and decades of leadership experience across continents and cultures, he distills it into seven bold, practical choices. These are not theories—they are tools. Tools to help you clarify what matters most, own your potential, move through fear, quiet the noise of other people's expectations, take action, embrace failure, and rise again when life knocks you down.

This is not a formula for perfection. It's a mindset for perseverance and growth.

In mountaineering, we often say the summit is only halfway. What matters even more is the journey back down to base camp and into life—the integration of what you've learned and how it changes the way you live. That's what this book offers: not just inspiration but integration. Not just a call to step up in big moments but a guide to practicing courage in the small, everyday ones.

Christopher's words invite you to see courage not as a onetime act but as a discipline—a muscle to be trained, a choice to be made again and again. And that's what makes this book special. It does not glorify a few heroic outliers. Instead, it elevates all of us. Telling us: *This is possible. This is ours to claim.*

So, wherever you are on your journey—at a crossroads, at the beginning of something new, or in the quiet moments of doubt—know this: you already have what it takes. You don't need to be fearless. You need only to begin.

I want to invite you to read this book with your whole heart. Let it challenge you. Let it steady you. And most of all, let it inspire you to live your life with more courage—every day.

INTRODUCTION

"Most men lead lives of quiet desperation and go to the grave with the song still in them."

—HENRY DAVID THOREAU

One afternoon in February 2017, in an industrial building located in the historic city center of Nuremberg, Germany, just thirty minutes by car from the global headquarters of adidas Group, about eighty of the company's top executives gathered. The hosts of the two-day offsite meeting were adidas' number two executive, who happened to be my boss, and...me. Our guests included the regional managing directors and global category general managers of adidas Group, along with the regions' heads of sales, retail, and marketing. Our goal was to refine and scale a new commercialization strategy I had developed.

I had joined adidas just two years prior, bringing to the company decades of experience in the sporting goods, lifestyle fashion, and retail sectors. The months leading up to my appointment had been tumultuous for adidas. The period was marred not only by a decline to fourth place in United States market share, behind bitter rivals

Nike, Jordan, and Converse,[1] but also by a public admission that a much-heralded, five-year global turnaround had not succeeded.[2] With its stock price depressed, investors irate, and leadership under pressure,[3] adidas shifted to a new strategy and sought fresh talent to drive it forward. I was part of this new guard.

Within weeks of joining the company, I was named Global Head of Key Cities, overseeing one of three pillars of the company's reinvigorated turnaround plan.[4] My responsibility was to develop and coordinate a brand and go-to-market strategy that would help The Three Stripes become number one in the most influential consumer markets for sports and pop culture—London, Paris, Shanghai, Tokyo, New York City, and Los Angeles.[5] Feeling the weight of lofty expectations, I focused on developing a plan, building a team, and rolling out an operating model. Over the next year, my city-led go-to-market model proved promising, and the Nuremberg meeting was critical for reviewing our initial efforts and expanding the initiative to other markets, beyond the initial six cities.

On the final day of the meeting, my boss, clearly delighted, took the stage to thank the participants. He spoke about the company's journey through a difficult period, adidas' Executive Board decision to pursue new leadership talent that could drive breakthrough strategic thinking for the company, and, specifically, me. He praised my courage for relocating from North Carolina in the United States to Bavaria, Germany, to join the company and expressed gratitude to my family for making the big transition with me. He also celebrated the ideas—such as the one we had met about—that my team had introduced since I joined.

This acknowledgment moved me deeply, as I had been working nonstop in the new role while privately ensuring that my wife and two young children were settling into life in a new country. My boss had been supportive, and yet I was touched by the unexpected public recognition.

His statement was more than just words—four months later, I was promoted to Senior Vice President of Global Sales for adidas Group charged with leading the company's global market and sales strategy as well as its worldwide marketplace development efforts.

By many definitions of the word, I was "successful." Far from my childhood and teenage years in my native Sierra Leone, West Africa, I had enjoyed a corporate career with US companies and was now a resident of Germany (and, at the time, as I came to learn, the senior-most Black executive at adidas). It had been an exciting journey and a prolific one. For my entire professional life, I had been breathing rarefied air, and I felt an interesting mix of humility and deservingness.

For many years, I had put in the study hours, earned the degrees, landed the jobs, made big contributions, and climbed the corporate ladder. By this time, I had lived and worked in eight cities in the US, Asia, and Europe and had held management and executive positions at some of the biggest names in consumer goods—Gap, Nike, VF Corporation, and now adidas. I had performed significant roles in business transformations, mergers and acquisitions, and brand initiatives that had delighted consumers and investors the world over. If I played my cards right, I was on my way to the C-suite, the ultimate culmination of a dedicated corporate career. I felt the momentum. I was ready, and it was thrilling…

However, only two years after that memorable meeting in Nuremberg, I walked away from it all.

NAGGING UNEASE

From the outside, my decision to retire from full-time corporate work seemed abrupt. You might be wondering how I could shift so quickly from an ascending career to simply walking away. The answer, briefly, is that I made the decision to reset my life's priorities and consequently take my professional endeavors in a new direction. I discovered something powerful—a stronger voice for my life's purpose that was not centered on reaching the summit of the corporate landscape. And, more importantly, I decided to act on it.

No, the shift did not happen overnight. It had started quietly a few years prior, with subdued notes which then grew into a crescendo that eventually filled every corner of my head, becoming impossible to ignore. In those years preceding, the tension had been building below the surface of my hectic professional life, persisting through milestones and accolades. No matter how successful I became, I couldn't shake the feeling that something was missing.

Sometimes, you may be living a decent life on the surface, but there's a nagging sense that something is amiss. Maybe things are not going as well as you want, but your instincts are pushing you toward the well-trodden path that has been known to work for others. Maybe your life is comfortable and stable, and you are hesitant to rock the boat by questioning things, even though you have a feeling those questions might lead to somewhere worthwhile.

Possibly, you feel all these things, not in relation to your profession or career but rather with how you are living your everyday life. Maybe you don't like the fact that you have too often opted for safety over adversity in your choices and decision-making. Maybe you know within yourself that you have never really stepped up to the plate and taken a risk at crunch time, or you have consistently fallen short when moments have challenged you to stand up or stand out from the crowd. Maybe you are a talented professional at work, but your personal life and relationships are in constant dysfunction. Or maybe you feel troubled and frustrated in the face of the world's overwhelming problems while still knowing deep down that you could make a real difference in other ways.

If any part of this resonates—the aversion to confront personal demons, the hesitation to rock the boat, taking refuge in the safe and familiar, the persistent whisper in your ears that there must be more than this—then stay with me. In finding my way to the other side, I discovered not just what was missing in my own life but also the lost note that might help you break free from what Thoreau called "quiet desperation" and finally compose the musical masterpiece you were meant to share with the world.

PRELUDE TO A SONG

To understand why I decided to walk away from corporate leadership exactly when I did, we need to look back further. The first notes of the melody began playing softly in 2012—when I was forty, but it took until 2018, six years later—for that melody to become more strident, introducing a theme that would become a full-blown symphony.

2012 was an eventful year in many ways. My wife and I were living in Kuala Lumpur, Malaysia, where I had been assigned to assist in the turnaround of Nike's Southeast Asia business (headquartered in Singapore) and at the same time manage the Malaysia market. It was fun work, even if I spent a considerable amount of time jetting between the two countries and traveling to the US and other markets in the region.

It was also the year my wife and I started a family and welcomed our firstborn.

As every parent knows, children give you a brand-new perspective on life. Sitting in the nursery in the maternity ward of Pantai Hospital in Kuala Lumpur, transfixed by my son's innocent little face as he gazed at the white walls of the stark room, I felt a rush of acceptance of my new title, Dad, and with this, a number of questions arose in my mind:

- What will my son's life be like, and how can I support his destiny?
- What changes will I need to make in my life to be a good dad?
- How will I want him to remember me?
- Will we become best friends and adventure together?

Despite this introspection and all the emotions that I was feeling, that was not my moment of awakening. Exactly twenty-four hours after my son's birth, I was back at work on stage in a ballroom of a golf club in the northern suburbs of Kuala Lumpur, opening a regional sales meeting for Nike.

I didn't act on my questioning thoughts in 2012. It did not feel like the right time, and I did not push myself to. I felt like I was poised to have it all. My career had tremendous momentum and was replete with future opportunities. All the key movements seemed to be playing in perfect harmony, and with a new baby, stability (defined as "don't rock the boat") was the highest priority. I did not break out into a full-throated song.

But something had changed, ever so imperceptibly. Softly, note by note, the questions had begun and continued playing in the background for a few years...until one powerful event brought things to a climax.

THE AWAKENING

My awakening came on the heels of 2017, arguably the best year of my career. As already mentioned, I was one of the key players in adidas' biggest strategic turnaround in recent years. My family and I were living in Europe and loving the experience. On top of that, I had recently been promoted and was making great money.

In late 2017, I was asked to help revitalize the company's biggest market in terms of revenue, where both our marquee brands, adidas and Reebok, were stalling. The stakes were high for the company and the entire regional organization. A new regional head had just been named, and together we drove the effort. With this new responsibility for the market's turnaround strategy, I gave it my all, even as I was learning about the different countries in the region and getting to know their teams. At the same time, the entire organization felt the stress to perform, and it was not bringing out the best in many of its senior leaders, making progress doubly difficult.

Then one weekend, right before an important regional go-to-market meeting, a senior member of the market executive team experienced a serious medical event, which shocked the entire organization. For me, in the thick of things, it was a fork-in-the-road moment that called for a massive reckoning. What if it were me? My children were too young to lose me. My wife did not deserve that either. The event also spurred a simple realization—with my personal journey and all my accumulated talents, I did not see a corporate appointment as my ultimate gift to the world or my role at adidas as the final, defining act in my profession or life.

It was clear. Something had to give. Would I continue to pursue the path of high-stakes executive leadership—chasing career and financial success, constantly in a death struggle with oversized egos—in my aspiration to the C-suite? Or was there another way—a healthier, meaningful, and joyful way to live?

I had come this far fueled by my dedication to excellence and the unwavering support of loved ones, especially my parents. They had made massive sacrifices for my siblings and me, all the while encouraging us to work hard and be the most accomplished and decent people that we could be. I'd also had a string of great managers who primed me for not only success but also impact. I had been the beneficiary of amazing mentors and diligent teachers who had drummed into me never to compromise who I was for success. Images and voices of all these supporters joined the cacophony in my head. These were the people who had always wanted the best for me and supported my growth toward my potential. I was certain that a premature demise on the hill to the corporate ivory tower was not the way many of them had envisioned my journey. I owed a lot more to all these people and to myself!

The questions that first arose at my son's birth started to repeat themselves but with more intensity and urgency.

Who was I? Professionally, I was a global executive with a Harvard education, an enviable resume and track record, and a vast professional network. But beyond that, what was I all about? What example was I setting for my children? I hoped that they would one day be proud of me, but I knew that I needed to be more *for them* and *to them*.

What did I have to offer the world? I had grown up overcoming limits of circumstance and opportunity and succeeded in reaching places I could not have dreamed of decades before. I have helped amazing brands and companies thrive and done so on many continents. *But was life in the corporate world my best gift to society or the best use of my talents?*

What was I leaving out? I was living in an intoxicating world of global movers and shakers, yet my roots were firmly planted in a modest African middle-class upbringing. The distance between these two worlds was vast, and even though both were near and dear and comfortable to me, *I increasingly felt like I needed to do a better job reconciling them within myself or risk not fully belonging in either.*

Which was a more worthwhile struggle—battling it out for professional turf or offering contributions and skills to causes that mattered to me and to people who would welcome my help?

Even more bluntly—was this me living my best life?

No!

That realization was a loud and final note in a crescendo that demanded a new dynamic to my life's symphony. It was time to seriously reconsider my choices. It was time to challenge the plotted course—to step away from the titles, the security, and the trajectory to the C-suite. It was time to define a new direction and veer into the unknown. It was time to walk away and perhaps risk the comfort, lifestyle, and perks my family and I had grown accustomed to.

Remember, all these thoughts were happening when I was at the peak of my earning years and a good two decades away from when I had thought I would retire. These thoughts were also upending career aspirations I had nursed since I was a teenager, the raison d'être of my life for thirty years.

So it was terrifying!

LIVING ON AUTOPILOT—SUCCESSFUL BUT UNFULFILLED

My inner turmoil wasn't surprising, and neither was my trepidation about acting on it.

In hindsight, I had been on autopilot for a long time—doing what I was "supposed to do." I had set a course for the mainstream definition of success and simply followed the obvious and well-trodden path toward it. When my instincts had forebodings about the path, I ignored them and pressed on. That's just what I thought one should do—stomach the costs of high advancement.

In Sierra Leone, my family was modest. We enjoyed life's basics, including strong values, a tough work ethic, and a loving relationship with each other, if not an overabundance of material possessions. We aspired, as do most families, for a better life.

However, not long after I was born, in the early 1970s, conditions in the country started declining, at first slowly, and then later at a rapid pace as poor leadership and political corruption spread. I learned early in life that my destiny had something to do with how hard I worked. And so I worked hard.

As a child, my vision of success was being the best I could be in any situation. It meant tenacity, giving my all, and adapting to fit changing circumstances. Only the best students got into the top schools. Only the top graduates got the best jobs. The best jobs would lead to guaranteed fortune and a good life. Being the best was the surest ticket to success, or so I thought. With the educational system in Sierra Leone eroding, the ultimate gateway to this glorious life was studying in the United States and, hopefully, one day achieving the American dream.

In 1991, I traveled to the United States on an academic scholarship to enroll at Morehouse College, a historically Black college in Atlanta, Georgia. As an immigrant handed a once-in-a-lifetime shot at my goal, the pressure to prove myself was baked into my psyche. I excelled at Morehouse and then did what you're "supposed to do" when you graduate from an esteemed college—I got a job with a big brand-name company. My career started to take off. First, I worked on Wall Street in investment banking with Lehman Brothers and Goldman Sachs and later with four leading consumer products companies.

Doing what I was "supposed to do" carried me a long way.

This is the real danger of living on autopilot: we set our course and focus on the next step and the next step only. Success and social pressures lead us to settle for normalcy, and sometimes we stay in this place for a long time, if not most of our lives. We lose touch with or never discover what else could have been—the unique dreams and other possibilities we could have explored.

Now, in 2018, I was thinking more deeply about my life, and the more I thought about it, the more I found a way to describe how I was feeling.

I was successful yet unfulfilled.

Anyone can get stuck in this mental place, no matter how old you are, where you come from, or where you are on your life's journey. This book is not about passing judgment—calling out what is good or bad about our lives or anyone else's journey. It is not about insinuation or vindication. It is more about a conversation, driven by self-awareness and reflection. You may still be on the path to professional growth—I am still on that path myself, so I'm not asking you to question your path. But how are you walking along the path, not just in your career but also more broadly? If you feel unfulfilled based on your choices to date and this concerns you, as it did me, I want you to ask yourself what's missing.

THE MISSING NOTE...COURAGE

When I eventually transitioned out of full-time corporate executive employment, I was three years shy of turning fifty, a milestone birthday that brings a clear acknowledgement that life's journey is well underway. It's the age when we joke about people going through a midlife crisis. What I experienced was midlife clarity—a valuable moment of reflection and application of acquired wisdom to plot a different path. I made a promise to myself as I left adidas—that I was going to pursue the rest of my life with more intention. With this awareness, I recognized there was something more I needed to discover—a new basis for living, even if I wasn't yet certain what that was.

So I took stock, not knowing what I would find or what I would do with my findings. I wanted my discovery to be based on me, my experiences, and the lessons I had learned from life. I retraced my long, winding journey up to that point. I thought about the decisions I had made and where those choices had taken me. I tried to remember events that were significant turning points or seminal moments.

Throughout this process, I wasn't frenetic or panicked or stressed (as a crisis would imply)—I was in deliberate and thoughtful retrospection in search of clarity. If I could step back and look at all the ups and downs of my life, I thought maybe I could spot something of salience, understand the bigger theatre I had been playing in and the audience I had been courting, and find a way to make my life a more beautiful musical score before it was too late. I asked myself:

- When I was at my best, what was driving it?
- When I fell short, what caused me to stumble?
- What wisdom have I gained over the years from working alongside and observing other professionals and leaders?
- What have I learned across cultures and geographies?
- If I could change one thing going forward, what would it be?

As these questions swirled in my mind, the answers emerged at first as a messy constellation of insights that slowly began to point in the same direction. As I dug for the root of my thoughts, a single word resurfaced repeatedly. Sometimes quietly, almost drowned out by other thoughts. Sometimes, and increasingly, loud and clear.

Courage!

When had I been at my best?

When I had shown courage.

When had I fallen short or disappointed myself?

When I lacked courage.

What had I learned from the myriads of people I met and places I experienced throughout my life?

It takes courage to live authentically.

It takes courage to be consequential.

It takes courage to pursue and live a fulfilled life.

What would I change if I had to do it all over again?

I would live life with more clarity, independence of thought, and intention.

I would seize more opportunities to make an impact, with courage.

I would prioritize being courageous over any other skill in life.
I would master the practice of courage.
That missing piece now had a name: *courage*.

ELUSIVE AND MESSY

You might have gone through periods in your life where you become consciously aware of unanswered questions and turn to books and other resources for help, as I did. But what you'll mostly find, especially in the business world, are books on how to develop strategy, be technically proficient, lead with charisma, be a great communicator, influence others, or navigate the world for effectiveness, often working within the confines of what is deemed acceptable to most people. Courage is glaringly absent, or given short shrift, in most business and leadership tomes I have read.

In Chapter 1, I will dive deeply into the concept of courage and share its definition. For now, though, I want to be clear—I was not completely lacking courage in the way that most people use the word. I was not a coward or afraid of everything.

When courage revealed itself as the missing note in my life's symphony, what I lacked was the diligent *practice* of courage. This is something deeper, something more intentional, and something more consistent. It's not just about occasionally being bold or performing awesome feats in certain moments; it's also about embracing life with more honesty and authenticity in both mindset and personal identity. And that was the key message—to grow through knowledge, self-awareness, and practice. By doing so, I would make the small decisions with ease, tackle the big ones when necessary, and do both with confidence. I would live a lifestyle rooted in purpose and principles that I would promote and defend while still making an impact.

I reached two realizations about courage early in this process:

First, that we each possess a unique identity and, with it, the *ability to make unique contributions to the world.* Unlocking this potential and fulfilling the promise of our most authentic self requires courage.

Second, that courage is not a biological trait but an *ability that's accessible to us all and well within our reach.* "Where there's life, there's a way," as the old proverb says. If you are alive, you are not disqualified from courage.

The truth is that we don't often view courage as something we can apply to our lives as a habit, and we don't often make the choice of courage. Imagine if we did—our abilities would increase exponentially. Courage could become our superpower, and yes, we would all have the choice to be superheroes in our own right.

Courage might seem like an ordinary concept, but it's surprisingly absent in our everyday lives. We don't talk about it, and we don't see it consistently in the actions of the people we're "supposed to" admire and emulate. Therefore, we don't prioritize it and practice it, and we suffer—both personally and collectively—as a result.

In whichever city or country you live, watch the news on any given day, and you will likely find yourself underwhelmed by political leaders. Just as I was finishing the final chapters of this book in 2024, the United States went through a presidential and congressional election season that was not only boisterous but also divisive. Citizens were disillusioned by the ballot options and, notwithstanding how the candidates wielded wealth, political power, and social influence, many of us felt *there was something missing from the picture, a picture that left us uninspired. Courage.*

Courage makes *a* difference.

Oftentimes, we stumble through moments where we know what's right but don't have the strength to act on it. We freeze in the face of unanticipated challenges and then look back with regret, wishing we had been prepared to do something. We allow opportunities for greatness to pass by, sometimes without even realizing it.

It's not that we never practice courage; we just do so sporadically. It sometimes happens by instinct but very rarely by design, and that's simply not enough. As Bronnie Ware shows in her powerful narrative, *The Top Five Regrets of the Dying*,[6] many people carry a sense of inauthenticity and unfulfilled potential all the way to their graves.[7] One of the top deathbed regrets she shares is "I wish I'd had the courage to live a life true to myself, not the life others expected of me."[8]

When I read that statement for the first time, something clicked into focus for me. I looked back at the turning points in my life and wondered: What were my true motivations? What expectation was I trying to meet? Who was I trying to please? Had I always risen to the moment? I knew I wanted to do better than others in Bronnie Ware's stories.

There *is* a way to escape this trap and reconnect with your true potential—and it's available to everyone, anywhere, at any time. To create a *life of fulfillment* and impact—we must have courage. And it takes a consistent commitment to making courageous decisions, both big and small, day after day.

Courage makes *the* difference.

THE PILGRIMAGE OF COURAGE

To gain more perspectives about courage, I interviewed scores of people, including leaders I had worked with and many individuals I have met along my life journey, some of whom you'll hear about in later chapters. I studied the works of philosophers. I read about the lives of folk heroes from around the world and throughout time. I checked in with ordinary people who I felt consistently displayed courage. I paid close attention to famous personalities and tried to zero in on what made them effective or not. I laid my own experiences bare so that I could test and validate the themes I encountered.

This book is the product of my reflections and explorations. Here is what I found about living courageously:

- It begins within.
- It moves us toward transformation.
- It is not linear and is fraught with uncertainty and challenge.
- It demands sacrifice, reflection, and commitment.
- It is deeply personal—and yet profoundly universal.

In these ways, the journey to courage bears all the marks of a pilgrimage.

Like any true pilgrimage, it begins with intention—not conscious at first but quietly persistent. A whisper in the soul that says, "There's more than this. There's a deeper way to live." For many of us, this call arises not in moments of triumph but in moments of discomfort: a leadership decision we avoided, a truth we didn't speak, a value we compromised. These are the thresholds that beckon us onto the path.

But courage does not come cheaply. It asks something of us. It demands that we walk—often uphill, often alone—through fear, failure, uncertainty, and doubt. It requires that we stop pretending and start paying attention: to our patterns, our narratives, our habits of avoidance, and, most of all, our choices.

In my work and in my life, I discovered that those who live courageously have not stumbled into it by accident. They are not superhuman (even if their courage makes it seem so). They have simply learned to master seven core choices—deliberately, with difficulty, and with dedication—as part of their daily lives, as part of their way of doing and being.

I use the word *choices* deliberately. Courage is a conscious daily act of becoming. And this is what also makes courage a pilgrimage. Think of the choices as stations on the routes of pilgrimage, points of revelation and discovery that anchor the foundation of courage. What is important is not that they are encountered in sequence but that they are experienced and mastered.

The seven choices that I defined are the foundation of this book. We will go through each one in its dedicated chapter. In summary they are:

- **Commit to a Purpose:** The essential fuel for courage is a goal, conviction, or vision you seek to achieve. The strength of this purpose will determine the strength of your motivation to be courageous. In Chapter 2, you'll see why this is essential and how to put a name to the thing that motivates you.
- **Own Your Potential:** Even with a sense of your purpose, you will inevitably meet situations or people that block your way. In those moments, you'll need to exude confidence, be your own chief advocate, assert your right to be your authentic self, and pursue your purpose. In Chapter 3, you'll see how easy it is to hold yourself back…and how to avoid that trap.
- **Unmask Fear:** Fear is the largest barrier that stands in the way of living your courageous life, because it emanates from both outside and within you. But is it real or just in your head? As you will find out, courage isn't about being fearless. It's about acting despite fear, which is exactly what you'll learn to do in Chapter 4.
- **Reject Distracting Voices:** We're bombarded with messages about what to think, what to do, and who to be—and most of them are unhelpful. Still, we care about how others perceive us, even if it means abandoning courage. In Chapter 5, you'll learn how to build your inner circle and disregard the voices and messages that can derail your progress.
- **Act Decisively:** Action is what turns good intentions into true courage, but too often, we let ourselves procrastinate and make excuses for our lack of action instead. In Chapter 6, you'll see

how to overcome those tendencies and train yourself to make action your default mode while also understanding the differences between inaction, wrong action, and helpful action.

- **Grow from Failure:** No one is perfect. We all make mistakes and fall short of our goals sometimes. This does not make failure any less scary or make us comfortable with failing. In Chapter 7, you'll learn that failure is in fact not all bad but part of the process of growth. You'll learn how to overcome damaging messages from your failures.
- **Embody Resilience (and Joy):** Courage will not come easy, and it is important not to give in or give out on this journey. Also, we live in a world that is not always fair, and it will sometimes feel like courage is a bigger risk for some more so than others. Chapter 8 acknowledges this and makes a special appeal to resilience and determination as alternatives to despair and surrender, and to never stop reaching for your potential.

As I mentioned earlier, despite being numbered in chapters in the book, the choices don't come in a prescribed sequence, priority, or required dosage, but they can be grouped in three ways.

- **The Accelerators:** The three choices that actively promote courage—committing to a purpose, owning your potential, and acting decisively. These are the choices to *fire up*.
- **The Decelerators:** The three choices to tackle our derailers of courage—fear, distracting voices, and aversion to failure. These are the tendencies that we need to *damp down*.
- **The Sustainer:** the choice to be resilient—*building* the stamina to stick with the messy journey toward courage.

COURAGE CONSTRUCT: ACCELERATORS, DECELERATORS AND SUSTAINER (ADS) MODEL

GROUP	C	O	U	R	A	G	E
Fire Up (Accelerators)	Commit to a Purpose	Own Your Potential			Act Decisively		
Damp Down (Decelerators)			Unmask Fear	Reject Distracting Voices		Grow from Failure	
Build Out (Sustainer)							Embody Resilience (and Joy)

WHO THIS BOOK IS FOR

To become courageous so that we can live without regret is one of the most meaningful pilgrimages a person can undertake and the biggest gift we can give to ourselves. And it must be owned completely. No one can walk it for us. There are no shortcuts. There is only the quiet, persistent work of becoming.

We may already be on this road without knowing it. I certainly was. My life is full of moments when I showed courage…and just as many when I fell short. But awareness was my invitation. I had to go back. Revisit decisions. Confront my fears. Reclaim my voice. And above all, I had to accept that courage was not about a single heroic act. It was about the small, consistent, conscious choices I made every day.

This book is one I wish I could have read many decades ago and reread throughout my life at critical crossroads or during periods when I felt any disquiet about the direction I was headed in. The choices speak to powerful forces that have played a role in all that I have been—an aspirational teen, a wide-eyed college graduate, an ambitious professional, a family man, and, today, a much more courageous leader and intentional person.

And it is for you—those who are starting off building careers and those who seek to be more effective as managers of people and teams and who are finding out that work must be done on the inner self to be effective as leaders. This book is also for senior executives who want to infuse courage into their organization's culture as they drive not only for success but also for lasting impact. The Courage pilgrimage is for everyone.

Regardless of where you are on your journey, I promise you that you can build elements of your life more courageously. This book might help you get there faster than I did, but that is not the goal. More importantly, I want it to help you get there in a healthier way, with fewer trade-offs and with a bigger toolkit to deal with the inevitable challenges and obstacles—not just in your career but in all facets of your life. Practicing courage is how we live without regrets, even as we enjoy a successful professional journey and passage through life, but "practice" is the key word. Like a muscle, we must continuously exercise it in everything that we do—all the time!

Throughout this book, you'll meet some *courage pilgrims*, a sampling of remarkable people who exemplify living a fulfilling and impactful life, one fueled by purpose and defined by bold actions. Some are famous or historical figures, but not all are. I have walked with my share of courage pilgrims over the span of my fifty years, and I know I will meet many more over my lifetime. In particular, there are seven individuals who have inspired me personally at different points in my life and with whom I reconnected as I wrote this book because they have strongly exhibited many of the traits I have written about in these pages—commitment to purpose, owning your potential, unmasking fear, rejecting distracting voices, acting decisively, growing from failure, and embodying resilience. Again, I am not positioning them as perfect people, but models who inspired me, and might you. You no doubt have many models in your own life, who are also inspirational to you and others.

At the end of each chapter is a Call to Action. We will cover a lot in this book, so I will use this section to zero in on a single next step. My brother Victor uses a simple trick he read about to keep himself focused. He decides every week—What is the *one* thing that I must accomplish? I use it here. I hope this approach guides you to action quickly.

FINAL WORDS—FIND YOUR SONG

What I offer here is no holy grail to solve all of life's problems. I am just one person, no different from you. These are simply ideas and techniques that I've found transformative in my personal experience and in firsthand observations of many people I admire. I don't ask you to adopt them without question—my hope is that they challenge reflections of your own and invite discussion with others like you—but I *know* they will be helpful as a road map on your pilgrimage.

I hope this book helps you search for your song, find it, begin singing it, and do so loudly. Thoreau wrote of lives of "quiet desperation," of people who go to the grave with their song still in them. This book is an invitation to defy that fate—to discover your melody, refine it, and perform it with courage so the world can hear it.

Before we can practice courage, we must first understand it. In the chapter that follows, we will begin by answering a simple but essential question: what exactly is courage? Chapter 1 will explore courage's true nature—what it is, what it isn't, and why it may be the most important skill you'll ever develop.

CHAPTER 1

THE HEART OF COURAGE

"Courage is the most important of all the virtues, because without courage you can't practice any other virtue consistently. You can practice any virtue erratically, but nothing consistently without courage."

—MAYA ANGELOU

My mother is an extraordinary woman. I make this statement with the understanding that it may be perceived as biased coming from her son; however, its source makes it no less true. She made an everlasting mark not only on our household but also on her vast extended family and friend network, including every community in which she spent time. Growing up, I was sure that the very least I could ever do for her was lay down my life—and I would do so without hesitation. Yet, in the summer of 1994, when a senior banker at Goldman Sachs made an inappropriate joke about her, I didn't lay down my life. Even worse, I didn't even defend her. I did nothing.

I had just completed my junior year at Morehouse College and landed one of a few highly coveted spots to intern at the firm. At twenty-two, I was the youngest on one of the trading desks, and like all the other interns at Goldman and across Wall Street, I hoped to secure one of the few even more coveted full-time roles available for fresh graduates the following year. This internship was my time to shine. With that in mind, I had been particularly studious all summer.

One evening, our entire department went out to dinner in SoHo, a trendy neighborhood in lower Manhattan, to celebrate a successful and substantial trade. In the middle of an otherwise pleasant meal, the conversation took a sharp turn when someone made a lewd joke about topless women, which was met with guffaws. I found it in poor taste and didn't laugh. Yes, I needed to ingratiate myself with my colleagues, but at the same time, misogynistic jokes and comments were not exactly my thing. My serious demeanor caught the eye of one of the more senior guys on the team, and, sensing a comedic opportunity, he somehow pivoted the joke to target bare-breasted African women.

"Christopher is wondering what's funny," he cracked. "He's thinking, 'I see my mom like that every day.'"

More hysterical laughter from around the table.

I froze, torn between shock (because I had not been expecting the attack) and humiliation (because this was about my mom—the selfless soul to whom I owed so much).

For a few seconds, I oscillated between embarrassment and anger. How dare they? I wanted to tell them that they were being offensive. I wanted to demand respect not only for my beautiful, strong, and tireless mother, toiling for our family thousands of miles away, but also for the continent and its cultures these guys clearly knew little about and had even less respect for. I wanted to decry their ignorance because I certainly had not grown up surrounded by bare-breasted women in Sierra Leone. I wanted to muster a comeback that would be equally offensive to them or sternly school them. I wanted them to understand that this conversation *was not okay in any respect*.

Then, in that split second, the pendulum that was my mind swung, and I thought about how desperately I wanted that full-time job. The ignorance and inappropriateness aside, a role at this company was everything I had worked toward for months. It was to be the crowning achievement of my undergraduate experience. I had earned a position there, and I knew that if I alienated a senior member of the team, chances were good that I wouldn't get it.

So I did nothing. I swallowed my pride, smothered my emotions, put on a straight face, and kept my mouth shut. The moment passed, and I'm sure no one else gave it a second thought. But I did.

For months after, I kept returning to that SoHo restaurant in my mind, confused and conflicted over what I should have done differently.

Should I have berated my colleagues for enjoying a hurtful joke at my expense? If I had, would they have written me off as oversensitive, with no sense of humor and, more importantly, not someone they could trust and want to work with on a long-term basis? Should I have reported the incident to the Human Resources department? Would anything have come of it? In those days, decades before Diversity, Equity, and Inclusion (DEI) initiatives and the #MeToo movement, this type of behavior was sadly commonplace on Wall Street. At bulge bracket investment banks, common decency was not a required quality. Making money for a firm was the ultimate sign of a person's worth, not their values or what they said around the dinner table, especially after they had just closed a big transaction. That aside, running to HR felt like an overreaction.

Should I have later, and privately, confronted the banker about it? Maybe, but even in private, there was a risk that saying something would place him on the defensive and sour him toward me, not to mention his advocacy for a job I desperately wanted. I could just hear his simple summation of me: "Not a team player"—that ambiguous phrase of death that is sometimes code for "not one of us" and has derailed many careers. None of these options felt right, yet what I did (or didn't do) couldn't have felt more wrong.

I've never told anyone this story and certainly not my mom. Ironically, I have a feeling that if I had asked her what to do at the time, she would have told me to do nothing. She would have told me that I did exactly what I needed to do in that situation—keep my eyes on the prize, let the insult go, and have faith. I always admired her for her courage, and I did exactly what I believed she would have counseled. And yet these thoughts did nothing to assuage the frustration, guilt, and regret I felt for a long time after. I could not see it as a courageous moment for me.

I recall this dilemma here because I have revisited this moment many times since it happened, and it raises several important questions that this book tackles.

What exactly is courage?

How do we choose between the many interpretations in society, across time, in literature, and in culture? Why does one decision or action feel courageous in one person but sit uncomfortably with another?

Why has my own life been dotted with so many moments and decisions of which I am proud and many others that I regret?

And why does a perceived lack of courage fill us with so much disquiet, as the Goldman Sachs incident did to me?

SHADES OF MEANING

Courage, bravery, fortitude, boldness, confidence, fearlessness, moxie, valiance, daring—these words often get used interchangeably, and their exact interpretations are, to a certain extent, up to the speaker or the listener. In everyday conversation, we might use "courage" to describe anything from someone wearing an outlandish outfit to another jumping into a swimming pool to save a baby from drowning. That may be fine for casual conversation, but to explore how to build a courageous life—one that will leave us feeling fulfilled—we need a deeper understanding of the concept and a much more specific and aligned definition.

When I started to research the idea of courage, I first explored my library of business and leadership books, but it was surprisingly absent from most of their lists of desired qualities. So I picked up a dictionary—a lot of dictionaries. As I read definition after definition, I noted some common threads. Several dictionaries defined courage as an "ability" to do something, implying that courage is a trait or a capacity. Many mentioned an "action" that arises from that ability or quality. So we can frame courage as an *ability to act*.

I also noticed that most definitions featured an element of *purpose*. I saw phrases like "achieve an end" and "to do something," indicating that a *goal* is involved—often described as "morally right" or "good," as well as "beneficial to the world" in some way. Some books subtly implied that the goal would be one of a "compelling nature" or of "significant impact."

Although none of the entries claimed that courage required a physical effort to achieve the goal, some mentioned a need for *mental strength*—that to be courageous, an "unpleasant deterrent or obstacle" needed to be overcome. Concisely, the goal would be difficult to achieve without special effort.

And while all the definitions I found mentioned "fear," "risk," or "danger," notably, none of them claimed that courage involved a *fearless* act. To the contrary, they all framed courage as the ability to withstand or control fear, or to act *despite* fear.

I looked up bravery too. The key distinction between bravery and courage lies in their nature: bravery typically refers to *instinctive* heroism, often as in physically dangerous situations, like firefighters rushing into a burning building without hesitation to save lives, where fear is suppressed by adrenaline. Courage, however, involves *deliberately calculating* risks before acting, making it a more reasoned response—while these concepts can overlap, with bravery potentially emerging from courage, courage isn't necessarily present in brave acts that stem primarily from impulse rather than careful consideration.[9]

The etymology of "courage" cements the idea that it is more intentional and deliberate. It first takes us to the French word, *le courage*, which typically means the "moral strength" to do something. In Old French, it was *corage*,[10] which derives from the Latin word *cor*, meaning...

Heart.

And so, "courage," even from its earliest origins, has always meant something deep within and unique to each of us because it emanated from the heart. It has never been a superficial trait or something merely driven by adrenaline. It is a quality or ability that is intrinsic to our core, as it originates from the depth of what makes us human, from our moral centers. Importantly, courage is a *universal potential* that resides within every individual, waiting to be harnessed. It is not reserved for a selected few but is a quality inherent in all of humanity, ready to be tapped into when needed.

THE PHILOSOPHERS WEIGH IN

Moving beyond dictionary definitions, the ancient Greeks and Romans embraced courage as one of the moral virtues. The Romans, for example, identified four main virtues they believed to be fundamental to their lives: *wisdom, justice, moderation,* and *courage*.[11] Not only is courage a cardinal virtue, but the *most important* virtue, according to Greek philosophers Plato and Aristotle. Without courage, they reasoned, one can't practice the other virtues, since courage is specifically related to facing fear.[12]

Among all the voices on courage in classical literature, I found

Aristotle's to be the loudest. He defined courage as an *excellence of the soul* that, through moral actions, could be cultivated and ultimately lead to a well-lived life.[13] He cautioned that the morality of courage is not based on fixed rules or laws but rather on one's own moral compass—on one's own true self.

I've used the word trait a couple of times. This is not to suggest that courage is genetic. For Aristotle, courage is a disposition that can be *refined with mindful practice.*[14] It is not an innate quality but a skill that can be trained up with good habits, leading to a stronger moral character. To develop the skill of courage, Aristotle recommends watching the courageous people around you and practicing doing what they do. Borrowing a page from Aristotle's playbook, I've included seven stories from courage pilgrims I've encountered on my journey. As you read the seven choices and each corresponding story, I hope you'll learn as much as I did about courage in action—happening in quiet but impactful lives.

Perhaps most famously, Aristotle believed that courageous people, like all virtuous people, avoid extreme behavior. Courage, then, is not the opposite of cowardice. Instead, courage falls on a spectrum between cowardice and rashness—what Aristotle calls the "*Golden Mean.*" While a cowardly person retreats from danger, and a rash person runs toward it thoughtlessly, a courageous person faces danger after thoughtful deliberation.

Fast forward a couple of millennia, and we encounter a whole different—but just as enlightening—take on courage. In the 1800s, existentialist philosophers like Friedrich Nietzsche were much more skeptical of any institution that dictated to people their place in the world. Nietzsche believed that instead of relying on broken institutions like social hierarchies or organized religion to guide us, we must each exercise our *free will* to find our own purpose.[15] Central to this process is the preoccupation that only through acts of courage—facing our deepest fears and challenging societal norms—can we uncover our true selves and live authentically, free from the constraints of external expectations.

In Nietzsche's view, finding a personal meaning of life, guarding it, and pursuing it—often in the face of opposition and criticism from others—requires courage. Self-determination is an act of creativity, a process of becoming who we're supposed to be. And, as we are becoming something different, we will have to overcome the pain, fear, anxiety, and difficulties of life that come with this growth.

COURAGE HAS VIRTUOUS INTENT

I need to belabor one point before I share my own working definition of courage. I found *virtue and morality* to be recurring, if not interchangeable themes, in the reflections about courage that I encountered. True courage does not degrade or exploit others. It serves our pursuit of self-actualization but not to selfish or oppressive ends. It presumes virtuous intent that leaves all concerned better off and often compels us to sacrifice or suspend our convenience if social good is in peril.

Every society has its folk heroes—from Che Guevara in Bolivia to George Custer in the United States, from founding fathers to freedom fighters—and most have legacies eulogized as courageous. I am not here to say who was courageous or not, but in researching this book, it was clear that there are multiple sides to every story, and the prevailing story depended on who was telling it, with the teller usually seeing themselves standing on the side of virtue and courage.

On my first full day of my first visit to South Africa about twenty years ago, our tour bus stopped at the Voortrekker Monument, a massive sandstone structure which sits atop a hill overlooking Pretoria, one of the capital cities It is dedicated to the Voortrekkers, the pioneers who migrated from the Cape Colony into the interior of South Africa in the nineteenth century. It is not only the tallest monument in South Africa but also significant as a cultural home for the Afrikaner people, representing their story from the Great Trek to the Anglo–Boer War. It symbolizes their heroism, perseverance, and a vision for the future. The walls also tell the story of December 16, 1838, the day the Voortrekkers defeated the indigenous Zulus at the Battle of Blood River. The monument took ten years to build and opened on December 16, 1949—the year after the apartheid government took power in South Africa.[16] At this point in the tour, my intellectual fascination with the monument gave way to question. In someone else's story, those murals were not celebrating courageous heroes. For many, these were not tales of virtue.

Given that we live in times where spin, semantics, counternarratives, word games, and alternative truths are part of our discourse, reshaping perceptions and definitions, I was mindful that the theme of courage and this book itself would not be distorted, misconstrued, and misused. I needed objective clarity of the concept in my definition.

But how do we evaluate whether our actions align with virtue in everyday life—not just in philosophy books? For me, one of the most useful frameworks comes from the Rotary Club. The club binds us, its members, to a code of behavior called the Four-Way Test "of the things we think, say, or do":[17]

1. Is it the truth?
2. Is it fair to all concerned?
3. Will it build goodwill and better friendships?
4. Will it be beneficial to all concerned?

I use the Four-Way Test much outside my Rotary life because I find it immensely helpful on this topic—are morality and virtue objective? For me they are, and the questions above have helped me define them. Again, this is *one* pragmatic lens that I use; you likely have yours.

It is here that I find the African treatment of courage also quite clear and especially resonant. Nelson Mandela embodied a form of moral courage rooted not just in personal conviction but in *Ubuntu*—a Nguni Bantu philosophy often translated as "I am because we are." Ubuntu emphasizes that our humanity is bound up in one another's, and Mandela lived this truth by choosing reconciliation over revenge after twenty-seven years of imprisonment.

"For to be free," he wrote, "is not merely to cast off one's chains, but to live in a way that respects and enhances the freedom of others."[18] That is *collective courage*—the kind that seeks justice for the many, even at great personal cost. It reminds us that courage is not just self-directed but other-centered.

Aristotle proposed that the *context* of an act further defines it as courageous. For example, a mercenary[19] (a soldier hired to fight for any country or cause), though facing grave danger, cannot be considered courageous because his *cause is not noble*. Because a mercenary is motivated only by profit, according to Aristotle, the moral component of courage is missing. But a soldier who sacrifices his life for a noble cause—like the freedom of his people—can indeed be labeled courageous.

WHAT COURAGE REALLY IS

From all this, we can more clearly see what courage *is not* and construct a confident definition of what *it is*.

Courage is *not* an extraordinary feat of bravery during which fear is suspended or ignored. It's not an act of bravado to impress others or feed selfish desires. It's not a rash choice to take a risk thoughtlessly or needlessly. It is not a rare trait reserved for the blessed or the lucky.

Courage comes from the *heart*. It is an act of self-determination fueled by a devotion that springs from the deepest part of the soul and psyche.

Courage is an *ability*. It can be learned by working on oneself, and it must be practiced.

Courage is a *moral virtue*. It reflects your values and serves others, not just yourself.

Courage is *deliberate*. It involves careful thought and intentional action.

Courage is *purposeful*. It is directed by a deep commitment to a goal or belief.

Courage is *uncomfortable*. It can only exist in the context of risk, challenge, and fear.

To sum it up in one simple sentence: *Courage is the ability to act intentionally in service of a virtuous core mission or purpose, despite the risks faced in doing so.*

DEFINING COURAGE

DEFINITION	CHARACTERISTICS
Courage is the ability to act intentionally in service of a virtuous core mission or purpose, despite the risks faced in doing so.	✓ Virtuous—motivated by fairness
	✓ Purpose-driven—guided by an ideal or principle
	✓ Deliberate—product of thoughtfulness
	✓ Active—projects out with intention
	✓ Defying—ignores conformity or acceptance
	✓ Uncomfortable—accepting of backlash
	✓ Heartfelt—independent; expressed authenticity

A WEE BIT MORE COURAGE, PLEASE

If courage is missing from our lives, it's sometimes because of a reluctance to go against the grain of what is considered acceptable, including social norms. Oftentimes we find ourselves in inexplicable moments where we know what to do, and we know how to do it, but we just don't. I observed and experienced this myself on many occasions, in life and career. Somehow, even when the stars are aligned—when managers have tons of work experience and support from their bosses, are resourced by their organizations, are given seniority and authority to wield, and surrounded by a willing team that follows them—they still fail to act in moments that demand inspiring leadership.

It takes more than all these things to be successful. Just a wee bit of courage is needed too, and this critical ingredient to living a life of impact is often missing.

This is what prompted me to sit unresponsively in that SoHo restaurant, the social cost to being different—and I am not alone. Most of us prefer to stay in the comfort zone of fitting in, even if that means saying or doing nothing when we feel we should.[20] When we succeed in fitting in, even if we still live well, we often nurse a deep sense of dissatisfaction, never becoming who we really want to be or, worse yet, never quite figuring out who that person is. We obediently follow what is expected of us while walking in the shadow of what we could have become. We may achieve many levels of success but feel that our lives lack joy.

Since I started doing more corporate board governance work, I have heard it said repeatedly that the most valuable trait for a Board Director is courage. You might wonder, "But why does this need to be said?" The volume of corporate malfeasance in the news over the last two decades is proof enough that our business leaders, like many of our political leaders, are not always great models of courage. Behind every failed corporation, there are executive leaders or a corporate board that also failed, in that they fell short on courage in some way.[21]

COURAGE IS A SUPERPOWER—GRAB YOUR CAPE

Once we gain a deeper understanding of courage and recognize it has its roots in the *heart*, we begin to have a different relationship with the word. We realize that courage isn't simply being a contrarian or going against societal expectations just because but being true to our own desire to live virtuously and authentically. We realize that courage is not an abstract concept, one too theoretical for practical people to understand. It is the journey to discovering who we really are, who we can become, and how we can make a lasting impact with our lives. We realize that courage is an incredible *superpower* that we all possess to do amazing things for ourselves and consequently, in the process, for others. Courage is a key that unlocks the inner us like nothing else does. Given that, why wouldn't we seek it relentlessly? And when we harness it, why wouldn't we use it regularly?

My favorite superhero is Batman, and in each movie in the eponymous franchise, there is a turning point when he descends into the Batcave, his subterranean lair, to prepare for a big mission. Nothing symbolizes Batman's otherworldly abilities to save the people of Gotham more than his cape. Not only is it a signature element of his imposing silhouette, but also, it's full of features that give Batman his superhero powers. We all have a cape of courage, but we don't reach into our closet and don it as much as we need to. We don't intentionally and extensively use the seven powerful choices that come with it either.

In today's world of seismic and unprecedented change, where leaders, policymakers, institutions, and governments suffer from ever-decreasing respect and credibility, individual courage seems more urgently needed than ever before. When I stepped into the role of President of African Leadership University in 2019, this awareness was etched into the school's ethos. Its curriculum is based on the seventeen Sustainable Development Goals codified by the United Nations in 2015. We taught our students that solving the world's most intractable problems will take courage, tremendous courage. So much so that the entire first year of every student's course of study focuses on their leadership core. So much so that the motto of African Leadership University is *Do Hard Things*.

When I lecture about strategy and transformation, I emphasize that leadership is about creating a positive impact, and this happens when we can lead teams and organizations to a vision. But to be effective at this, managers must first learn to lead themselves with courage.

Courage is essential to pursuing self-leadership. Yet somehow, many leaders have still not figured this out. Or they do not want to do hard things!

I will go a step further. In the increasingly social media-driven society we have become—where opinions get communicated and disseminated at record speed and where tribes form quickly within echo chambers—we are prone to judge and be judged endlessly. Consequently, we need to exercise courage more consistently just to stay sane and to protect our individualism and independence. With this understanding, three important conclusions concerning courage rise to the surface:

1. Courage can transform how we live and the legacy we leave behind. It is a *superpower* we can harness in more transformative ways than other traits.
2. We cannot live fulfilling lives without practicing courage. Courage needs to be a more integral part of who we are. It needs to be a comfortable tendency, often *second nature*.
3. Courage can be *learned* and is accessible to each one of us. Courageous people are not a rare breed. We all have it within us to grow in courage, so long as we commit to it. We all have that cape tucked away somewhere within reach. This is great news.

BUILDING COURAGE IS A MESSY PROCESS

When I started interviewing people for this book, I was surprised at how hesitant many people were to describe themselves as courageous, even those whom I found to be so. Courage, it seems, is something we would rather have others say about us than claim for ourselves. It is no wonder then that it is not explicitly highlighted as other traits are in leadership books, even though it seems to undergird the greatness of consequential people. In business, people often say that you cannot achieve what you don't measure. We can say the same for our abilities. We cannot achieve what we do not practice.

Because I describe courage as a skill, you may find yourself believing that courage requires perfection. But this way of thinking only sets you up for disappointment. Courage cannot be measured on a precise grid. Courage is not the heroic process of becoming fearless or learning how to be so. It's not about standing up against the status quo every chance you get or picking reckless fights with anyone and everyone you disagree with. It is not about having the absolute best answers and solutions to everything or executing them flawlessly all the time.

Inherently, building courage is messy. It is not just about choice-making but also about exercising judgment. Often you will make mistakes and undergo trial and error. You will struggle. The struggle is part of the process.

I can think of few greater examples of an "ordinary" human struggling with fears, doubts, and extreme opposition while demonstrating superhuman courage than Abraham Lincoln. Throughout his political career, Lincoln vacillated on the issue of slavery, often wrestling with its myriad moral and political complexities. He was not consistently courageous, but he was consistently working at it. Ultimately, his commitment to preserving the Union and his increasing belief about the moral and ethical imperative to end slavery culminated in some of the most decisive and bold actions ever taken by any American.

Prior to the Civil War, Lincoln publicly spoke against the expansion of slavery into new territories. Yet, despite being accused of being an abolitionist by his political opponents, he did not advocate for the eradication of slavery where it already existed. As the Civil War raged on, Lincoln's stance evolved. He recognized that ending slavery was not only a moral necessity but also essential for the country's very future. This realization led to the Emancipation Proclamation in 1863, an unprecedented executive order mandating the freedom of slaves in Confederate states.

Lincoln's courage then propelled him to push for the passage of the Thirteenth Amendment to permanently abolish slavery throughout the United States. His resolve, despite extreme political and personal risk, marked him as a leader willing to sacrifice everything for the principles he believed in.

Tragically, these bold actions led to his assassination shortly after the Civil War ended. Upon his death, Frederick Douglass, a former slave and leading abolitionist who had often been a thorn in Lincoln's side, eulogized him in his death. Douglass acknowledged Lincoln's complex journey and his greatness. He praised Lincoln not just for the emancipation of slaves but for his ability to grow and act with courage in the face of immense pressure and opposition. His words were a testament to the idea that true courage involves growth, complex decisions, and the willingness to act boldly for the greater good, even at great personal cost.

Perhaps you're thinking right now that you're not Lincoln; you're not superhuman. But I remind you that he wasn't Batman either; he was a man with the same doubts and fears you and I have. The actions he took despite those doubts and fears is what we're talking about and what we can all do when we practice courage.

THE PROMISE OF A LIFE WITHOUT REGRET

You also may be asking why you should bother. What's the big deal? Why shouldn't I just continue to live my life as I have been—staying within my comfort zone and not stressing out by rocking the boat?

My answer is this: that is a choice you can certainly make. At the same time, I know that there are other choices, the one of courage being one that I promote. You should build courage because that's how you rise to meet moments in your life that realize your highest potential and define your unique purpose. You should do it because that's how serving your purpose helps you in finding lasting fulfillment. It's how you build a life you're proud of and minimize regrets over opportunities not taken. It's how you get to the end of your earthly journey and feel satisfied that you made the most of your time in this realm. Ultimately, the practice of courage is how you make the world a better place in the ways that mean the most to you.

Personally, I have found immense joy in shifting to live courageously and embarking on the journey to find my courageous self. There is so much liberation in seeking, finding, and claiming your own agency and not letting others or circumstances dictate your life for you. In addition, if we are to maximize our other virtues, make a positive impact on the world, or live genuinely happy lives, then we must first unlock our courage.

With courage, you reclaim your agency. You no longer live by default but by design. That shift alone can change everything.

THIS JOURNEY IS NOT FOR THE FAINT OF HEART

As for me, I did not receive a full-time offer from Goldman Sachs in the summer of 1994 (but I did return to Wall Street at another firm). So, as it turns out, pushing through my fear and practicing courage that summer evening would not have hurt my career after all, despite those very real concerns in my mind at the time. However, letting that fear guide my decisions and dictate my actions that evening left me dissatisfied with myself in some respect and still regretful thirty years later.

Had the incident happened today, that banker and I would have had a nice private chat. I must steal a page from the literary classic *Pilgrim's Progress*.[22] In the book, the pilgrims Christian and Faithful walk into the town of Vanity Fair knowing they don't belong and anchored in who they are. They display unwavering humility as strangers but still speak plainly about their beliefs—even when clashing with local customs, inciting scorn or persecution.

In hindsight, I entered Wall Street like a novice pilgrim arriving at an unfamiliar town—ambitious, hopeful, and unaware of the test ahead. But I still don't think I would have done things differently in 1994—I was too unprepared, too young in my career, and the decks were too stacked against me. When the moment came to speak up, I stayed silent, letting the values of the place shape me.

Pilgrims learn by walking, and I have since learned that not all silence is peace, and not all belonging is worth the cost. True courage comes not from fitting in but from staying true—especially when it's hard. My younger self chose not to fight that battle and risk perishing. My older self is authoring the book I wish I would have read then.

As you can see, courage is a pilgrimage and a messy one at that. Self-awareness is critical, as is resilience, both of which we will talk about in coming chapters. That said, the memory of that evening in SoHo still unsettles me.

FINAL WORDS—YOUR FIRST CHOICE

C.O.U.R.A.G.E. isn't just my story. It's yours too. Deciding whether to start this journey is your choice to make. Pause for a moment and think back: When have you stood at a crossroads where the easy path conflicted with the right one? What choice did you make?

This book is an invitation not only to read but to reflect. As you move forward, keep that moment in mind. It will become your anchor as we explore what courage is together.

Along your journey to live a courageous life, you will certainly experience a range of emotions and challenges like I have. It may start with a feeling of *discontent* with the status quo or a role being forced upon you. You may feel dissatisfied with the world around you and with the person you are in that world. Engage that discontent, as it is discontent that drives the very change needed.

Also, this journey will not be televised or heralded. By that I mean that as you evolve and begin to think, speak, and act contrary to your old life, not everyone will understand your private reflections and new choices. Some will be critical. As such, you will need *discipline* and *self-mastery*. You must be the master of your inner voices—listening carefully to your heart and knowing how you feel each step of the way.

And although it may go against what you've been taught, a little *shamelessness* is a good thing. Feeling shame will stop you from breaking away from the crowd and stepping out of your comfort zone. In a society that often praises conformity, you must be confident *and* shameless in the actions that will boldly send you in your own direction.

Finally, you may experience inexplicable *cheerfulness*, a giddy feeling as you tackle this wild, fun journey of becoming your own person, one for whom courage is second nature. Embrace this feeling of liberation and joy. In fact, relish the whole journey.

Good luck on your journey. You are ready to make your first choice—taking the first step and setting the course to our north star—courage. In Chapter 2, we will explore what it means to commit to a purpose.

A CALL TO ACTION: TRAVEL YOUR PILGRIMAGE LIKE AN ATHLETE

I know. Pilgrimage and athlete—strange combination, but I mean it. On this journey, approach courage like an athlete approaches excellence: train deliberately, track your progress, and expect discomfort as part of growth.

THE GOAL OF THIS CALL TO ACTION

Begin the process of intentionally building courage as a skill by shifting your mindset from passive reflection to active training. Just like athletes improve with daily practice, repetition, and a support system, your courage grows when you engage it purposefully and consistently.

HOW TO BRING IT TO LIFE

1. **Start immediately:** Set a small, clear goal this week that requires you to act with courage—speaking up, setting a boundary, or standing for your values.
2. **Do the reps:** Repeat your courage-driven actions in real-life situations, even when imperfect. Practice is progress.
3. **Track your performance:** At the end of each day or week, reflect—what did I try, what did I avoid, and why?
4. **Curate your mental inputs:** Avoid narratives or environments that dilute your focus. Feed on positive stories, role models, and voices that inspire courage.

KEY ENABLERS OR CHALLENGES TO BE MINDFUL OF

- **Discipline beats inspiration:** You won't always feel motivated—build the habit anyway.

- **Mindset matters:** You're not training to be perfect; you're training to be ready.
- **Protect your energy:** Surround yourself with mentors and peers who fuel your growth.
- **Expect resistance—from within and from others:** Like an athlete pushing limits, discomfort is the sign you're in the arena.

Your courage will grow in the same way as an athlete's skills do—through steady, intentional training. Step onto the track, take the first rep, and let each deliberate action move you closer to the courageous life you're building. Prepare to get fit!

CHAPTER 2

COMMIT TO A PURPOSE

"The two most important days in your life are the day you are born and the day you find out why."

—MARK TWAIN

My favorite interview question to ask job candidates (or to be asked when I am a candidate myself) is "What motivates you?" The answer helps me understand what truly makes people do what they do, and what kind of drive and energy they will bring to a team once hired. Having the drive to succeed is a powerful contributor to the dynamics of a high-performing team, so this question often tells me more about them than the other questions on my list.

Likewise, courage is driven by a powerful sense of commitment to, or conviction about, something.

While the answer changes over the course of each person's life depending on the circumstances at any given time, I have found that a core motivation fuels each of us. Often this stems from powerful crucibles—searing experiences—in our childhood, defining events or important priorities in our lives, but this is not always the case.

Regardless, this kernel lives within us and understanding it could be key to our quest to live courageously.

Our core motivations take different forms for each of us and evolve at various stages of our lives. You already know a little about my birth story and early years. When I was much younger, I was driven by mostly school-related goals that I had set for myself. In adulthood, I started to drive toward a purpose instead, and even that evolved over time. I had obviously grown wiser and benefited from more life experiences. Either way, courage needs something to work for, so knowing what drives us is critical to the process of becoming courageous. As one matures on the courage journey, the urge, and the need, to graduate in aspiration and define a higher purpose will grow stronger.

By way of illustration, someone who grows up in poverty could be driven by the core motivation *never to be poor again*. This determination could fuel much of their life and drive many of their choices and decisions. But over time, a bigger life purpose could emerge, and it would be something that transcends merely "not being poor." In this example, it could become a mission *to eradicate homelessness in their community* or a commitment *to be a voice for the hopeless and the helpless*.

The bottom line is it's hard to be courageous if we don't care about anything. And the depth of our courage will depend on *how much* we care about something. I am not suggesting that a grand life mission will shape all our decisions. We make hundreds of decisions and choices every day, and most are in service of simple goals that we have set to meet immediate or everyday needs, like "I will shop for furniture at store A versus store B because store A better suits my budget and style." But even here, clarity about budget and style creates constraints that not only define the goal but also make a final decision more grounded and, frankly, easy. Goals that we set for how we want to live or experience life day by day help us make better decisions in the moment. In the same way, our core motivation and purpose will help us make better big-picture decisions about our lives that are aligned with our intrinsic needs and lead to more fulfillment. If we serve them faithfully and with conviction, they will help us practice courage to live our best lives and make our own unique mark on the world.

I myself have had different core motivations at every stage of my life, but the central themes have been clear even if they evolved over the years. They were spawned by early life experiences, which shaped or influenced most of my goals and today are the foundation of my current expression of purpose.

My purpose is to be a catalyst for positive change by inspiring courage in others. In everything I do, I seek to leave an impact on others that outlasts me.

It's a bold statement—and I mean it. More importantly, how did it come about?

DREAM AUDACIOUSLY

In the mid-1970s, Sierra Leone had, and still has today, a single international airport, Lungi. Freetown, the capital, is located at the tip of a peninsula and Lungi, across the water on the mainland. Which means that the airport is difficult to reach. The distance wasn't far, but the travel options available at the time were unreliable and accident-prone. And traffic on the one rugged road there could be so bad that it was common for travelers to start their journey to the airport ten to twelve hours before their flight. On top of the logistical nightmare of getting to the airport itself, flights only arrived and departed every few days, and most citizens had neither the means nor the need to travel abroad. So going to the airport was rare and therefore quite an event.

Once, when a family friend had to travel to the United Kingdom, my parents decided we should make his send-off a family field trip. Together, both households took the long journey on the ferry and arrived at Lungi with plenty of time to share a nice meal in the visitor lounge on the upper floor of the terminal. But I couldn't care less about the food because I was entirely captivated by the massive sleek British Caledonian airplane sitting on the tarmac one hundred meters away. I had seen planes in the sky but never up close. It was longer, taller, wider, and shinier than anything my five-year-old imagination could have dreamed up. I stared at it, transfixed, throughout the meal.

Eventually, a buzz swept through the airport as takeoff time approached. We stood on the balcony in the send-off area and watched as the passengers, including our "uncle," started toward the plane, walked up the stairs, and disappeared inside. Then the steps were towed away, and, for what felt like an eternity, the plane just stood there. Finally, it started moving slowly, rolling down the runway away from the terminal, then turning to the right and slowly out—so far away that I could no longer see or hear it taxiing. I wondered if the show was over. Suddenly, the engines roared to life in the distance. Within moments, the plane approached then sped past the terminal building, a silver blur throwing off hot wind and making a deafening noise. As if by magic, with its noise fading quickly, it was lifting nose-up into the sky and tucking its wheels in with bird-like grace, leaving a white cloudy trail in its wake.

At that moment, something ignited in me. My parents had raised us to be curious about the world and to see the globe as an arena which we were free to explore and thrive in. One day, we could use our knowledge and experiences to contribute to Sierra Leone's future. At that moment, in that airport terminal, I was witnessing the gateway to this enthralling possibility. At that moment, I formed my first visceral life aspiration.

I decided that day at the airport *I wanted to soar just like that jet and go wherever it went. I wanted to spend my life exploring, learning, and growing.* That has been my core motivation to this day. And it has never wavered.

TURNING DREAMS INTO REALITY

In the decade before I was born, both my parents went to the United Kingdom on colonial government scholarships, my dad to train as a marine engineer and my mom as a corporate secretary. But when the independence movement gained momentum in Sierra Leone, they returned home early, excited by the promise of a new self-governing republic and the roles they would play in it.

Unfortunately, events did not unfold as they expected. Postindependence, the country was marred by political rivalries, then rampant corruption, and the economy fell apart. The dreams of how they would raise their family, which once had been within my parents' grasp, diminished and eventually disappeared out of reach.

Undeterred, their focus turned to their children. They gave my siblings and me the best education they could afford and made sure we did well in school. They introduced us to the world through books and the radio, where broadcasts from the British Broadcasting Corporation and Voice of America were a window into a presumably more functional and promising outside. They wanted us to know life beyond the limits of our place of birth and their means.

Until that day at the airport, my entry point into the big world had been unclear and seemed like a fantasy, the figment of a child's imagination and my parents' empty dreams. But now, I knew for sure that it was real, and I desperately wanted to discover it for myself.

As you can see, even as a young boy, my desire to explore ran deep. My core motivation wasn't travel. It was breaking through barriers and challenging limits. It was proving to myself that I could do anything, as our parents had always assured us. This was when I first encountered the concept of potential—that invisible yet ever-present force, a height of achievement, within reach if only I strived for it. My job was to find it and grab it. Years later, at Morehouse College, I discovered that one of the school's most illustrious presidents, Benjamin Elijah Mays, had already captioned my mindset, "Not failure, but low aim, is sin."

Today, if I were to map out my footsteps on a globe, there would be dots on nearly every continent. Notably, I've officially lived in fourteen cities across four continents. But I haven't just moved around physically. I've also traveled intellectually, mentally, and emotionally through organizations, states of change, and diverse contexts. I've been employed by eight entities in all, including Custament Partners, the consulting practice I founded and currently run, and have taken on dramatically distinct roles and assignments at each one.

No one forced me to do any of it. I made a majority of those moves at times when I didn't need to change anything—at times when my life was good—in whatever city and country I was in. These choices often surprised the people around me (and my mom), who wondered why I didn't just stay in one place like everyone else. These moves were driven by my core motivation, not just to learn new things but to learn radically different things. I believe that I can only learn when I do something new and different—something that forces me to engage with new realities—like moving to another country or company.

When learning plateaus, I feel the pull to soar again—to break new limits; a relentless curiosity about things and the quest for new knowledge and experiences is a powerful force in my life. Over time, this motivation led me to discover my life's mission and purpose.

FINDING PURPOSE (IT'S NEVER FAR AWAY)

I know exactly where it started, when my core motivation started evolving into a fully formed purpose: Morehouse College.

The alma mater of Dr. Martin Luther King, Jr., has a proud tradition of producing men of consequence. Sometime in my first year, it hit me how fortunate my life was. Notwithstanding the economic and physical hardship of growing up in Sierra Leone, I had many blessings—parents who encouraged me, teachers who nurtured me, a high-quality education, a community that was proud of me, and extended family who doted on me. I had role models who directly and indirectly nudged me toward my potential through every interaction with them. This rich reservoir of supporters grew at Morehouse. By the time I graduated and started my first job at Lehman Brothers, it was clear to me that community and education had been important accelerants in my life.

Still, Morehouse touched me even more profoundly than this. After four years of eye-opening exposure—studying the people and events that had transformed societies the world over, it became impossible not to reflect on my own responsibility to drive positive change for others. And any type of change, I learned, begins with the individual.

In my junior year, the Economics and Business Administration department launched a mentorship program and paired a few students with community leaders. This was pre-internet, and I did not know anything about the local doctor who agreed to mentor me. I was curious why an Economics major hell-bent on working on Wall Street needed an orthopedic physician as a mentor. However, Dr. Hamilton E. Holmes was no ordinary doctor, or person, for that matter. He, together with a lady named Charlayne Hunter-Gault, were the first African Americans to integrate the University of Georgia. In addition, Dr. Holmes was the first African-American student to attend Emory University School of Medicine, where he earned his medical degree in 1967, later becoming a professor of orthopedics and an associate dean at the school. Dr. Holmes (now deceased) and I had several conversations, and what I remain struck by until today was his acceptance of his calling to do hard things and his personal humility about his successes.

It's hard to spend time with someone like Dr. Holmes, a heavyweight in the US civil rights narrative, and then continue on with life as usual. I already had a thirst for exploring, learning, and growing, but in the years at Morehouse, I was awakened to a sense of gratitude for my own good fortune and a strong awareness that positive influences and education had fueled it. I also became keenly aware of those who did not have my opportunities and resolved that the least I could do was help them in their own paths. I still wanted to soar but also help others grow their wings and soar too. In any way I could, I would be a catalyst focused on leaving a positive and transformational impact on their lives. I do not know the exact date, but it is safe to say that while at Morehouse, I experienced that second important day in your life that Mark Twain talked about. That conviction has shaped my choices since.

I know you will find your purpose in your own time and manner. Your situation will be different and your purpose uniquely yours. Often, even those closest to you may not understand what it is and how or why it comes about, and that's okay. Listen to your heart and follow your instincts, for they will guide you to the cause to which you will devote your life and your gifts.

There is something else about purpose. It is not enough to have one; it is also important to feed it and nourish it. Sometimes, it takes time for your purpose to deepen and for you to allow it full access to your life—letting it shape your decisions and influence the person you become. This is why we are talking about purpose now at the beginning of your journey. Purpose is the essential fuel that will direct all your courageous actions. In fact, true courage is hard to harness without it.

In my travels, I have been fortunate to meet others whose journeys have inspired mine, as I hope mine inspires yours. I am sharing the stories of these courage pilgrims in each chapter called Courage Pilgrims in Action.

COURAGE PILGRIM IN ACTION
ALI HASSAN MOHD HASSAN (PHILANTHROPIST)

"I try to do as much good for the youth as I can with the gifts that I have been blessed with."

Over the burgeoning sports business landscape in Malaysia, one company reigns supreme. Independently owned al-Ikhsan Sports was founded in 1993 and grew to about two hundred stores over three decades. In the process, it became a go-to destination for all things sportswear-related for millions of consumers.

With its commanding share of the market, three facts make the al-Ikhsan story fascinating: It is the most beloved sports retail brand in one of Asia's most important sports-obsessed markets, serving Malaysia's twenty million fitness enthusiasts. It has been successful in fending off better-known and better resourced competitors, who have tried for years to unseat it from its perch. The company grew organically from a fifty-ringgit (twenty-dollar) investment by founder Ali Hassan Mohd Hassan and his wife.

Ali Hassan, a humble and soft-spoken man, is an idol for ethnic Malay youth. He grew up in a pious, working-class Muslim family. Though he dreamed of becoming a world-class footballer, financial constraints led him to pursue mechanical engineering on a scholarship at Universiti

Teknologi Malaysia. Sacrificing personal ambitions, he used his scholarship money to support his family. After graduating in 1993, Ali turned down an opportunity for further education abroad, choosing instead to start a business selling sports equipment.

Today, Ali Hassan is one of his nation's most highly regarded businesspeople, admired for his successful strategy of maintaining low prices to make branded sports products accessible to youth with dreams like he once had. His empire has included partnerships with global brands such as adidas, Nike, Puma, Umbro, and Liverpool Football Club. A critical element of his story is that he has not forgotten how it felt to grow up poor. Through his business and personal charity, he supports young people in pursuing and realizing the dreams he never could. Beyond business, Ali is a committed philanthropist and motivational speaker, donating generously to the community and inspiring aspiring entrepreneurs nationwide.

I asked Mr. Hassan how he found the courage to resist the high-pressure tactics of larger partners, despite the often-punitive impact on his business. He was as resolute and affable as ever. His faith had given him purpose, he said, to promote peace in the world with charitable deeds and to seek rewards not on Earth but in heaven. The object of his energies—young people, whose lives he hopes he transforms permanently with his ever-growing business and charity work. They fuel his purpose, the source of his courage—to keep dreaming and expanding—and his fortitude to withstand the Goliaths who have sought to stop him over the years.

He says, "My faith is my guide. It teaches me to do as much good as I can, and that is a commitment that I inherited from my parents and that I have made to God. Difficulty is a path to growth, so I regard it as positive. The enjoyment of giving and not expecting anything back makes me happy. It promotes more happiness and peace with kids, and that is the way of Islam."

Years ago, when I was ending a two-year assignment as Nike's Malaysia General Manager, Ali wanted me to visit with him one final time. As I left his office after lunch and a few hours of friendly conversation of reminiscing and mutual praise, he got up from his seat, walked over to his desk and picked up something. He shook my hand and pressed a parting gift into it. I was touched. He was sending me off with the one thing that had most fueled his purpose. It was a copy of the Quran.

PURPOSE VERSUS PASSION (AND WHY IT MATTERS)

These days, especially in America, passion is *en vogue*. You hear people talk a lot about finding their passion and pursuing it, so is that what we're talking about here? *Is* passion the same thing as purpose? For some people, like my sister Harriette, it is.

She is a policy specialist in peace and security with UN Women with the official title of Head of the Compact Secretariat. But well before her United Nations role, she worked to foster gender equity for two decades in many developed countries and hotspots in the world, from Sudan to Afghanistan to Burundi. Being the capitalist and doting big brother I am, I have tried to lure her to the corporate side, where I know she could land a lucrative role at the helm of a corporate foundation. But for years she has been adamant—that the UN is where she has the biggest platform and strongest mandate to impact the most women around the world, and she would rather stay true to the quality of her impact than have a comfortable job without much opportunity to leave a legacy. She lives both her passion and purpose each day.

Purpose and passion can certainly overlap, but there's at least one important distinction. Passion refers to a *high intensity of feeling for something*—excitement, enthusiasm, zeal. That usually comes from the intersection of what you love and what you're good at.

This enthusiasm can lead to a deep commitment, even a lifelong devotion to a subject, one that gives you energy. But there's one thing missing—*direction*.

Purpose, on the other hand, is grounded in value and points you toward a desired outcome. That comes from adding one more element to the mix—not just what you love and what you're good at but also *how you want it to impact the world*. Purpose strives to fulfill a need, one that goes beyond your individual self. It embodies the change you'd like to see in the world. Purpose comes from a deeper understanding of one's core motivation crystallized in a vision. In short, purpose is passion applied to meaningful change in the world.

I have a love (you can call it a passion) for traveling and experiencing unfamiliar cultures, but my deeper mission (my purpose) is to help others transform, both personally and professionally. While my passion for travel fuels my energy and excites me, my purpose lies in fostering change, wherever in the world I find myself—whether for individuals seeking personal growth or companies aiming to transform. That mission shapes my career choices—from strategic planning to brand management to board governance.

My purpose has also compelled me to write this book. Yes, writing is a passion of mine, but writing about the topic of courage has a lot more to do with my purpose. For your purpose to be meaningful to you it must also overlap with your passion...Why wouldn't it?

PURPOSE AS FUEL

According to a study by McKinsey only about 55 percent of adults can actually articulate their purpose. In addition, 70 percent of people say they define their purpose through work.[23]

Think about that. About half of us aren't sure *why* we're doing the things we do. That doesn't mean we've all completely derailed. We might be cruising along simply fine, holding down jobs, raising families, and enjoying professional success by many standards. If most of us are perfectly functional without a clearly defined purpose, it begs the questions—Why do you need one? What difference would it make?

It's an issue of choice. Every single day, we have countless decisions to make. Are we going to spend time on this activity or that one? With these people or those other ones? What are we going to spend money on, what are we going to wear, what are we going to eat, what are we going to say? And on and on. And sometimes, we'll have much bigger decisions to make, with far greater impact than what we are wearing or eating for lunch, such as whether and when to take a job, buy a house, get married, or have children.

Without purpose, we default to convenience or others' opinions. Choices will get made, no doubt, but they probably won't complement each other, and they almost certainly won't add up to a fulfilling or impactful life. Your purpose helps you steer your life in the direction you want to go, decision by decision. Purpose aligns choices, big and small.

In addition to giving us clarity and direction, purpose gives us stamina. Those without a purpose are more likely to crumble when they meet challenges. As you learned in Chapter 1, courage is purposeful by its very definition. For an action to be courageous, it must be in service to some deeply held mission. Courage also inherently involves some risk or discomfort. It's never an easy option. Unless you have a strong purpose driving you to take the courageous path, you probably won't do it. Instead, you'll settle for the comfortable path—the path of least resistance.

In that way, purpose is essential fuel for your courage. It gives us both the reason and the strength to make courageous choices—our very motivation to move forward. Those are the choices that add up to a life aligned with your true self, where you fulfill your potential and make the impact that matters to you.

A sense of purpose isn't just some grandiose, philosophical idea. It has practical, daily applications. It empowers you to approach each situation with clear criteria to help you make even some of the smallest daily decisions. Being aware of your purpose will naturally lead you to consider: What do I want to get out of this activity? How does this relate to the bigger me?

Instead of simply showing up to our jobs each day and crossing tasks off our lists, a sense of purpose leads us to examine our work more deeply. We'll start to ask: Where do I want to work and why? What will I do? How do I want to work? How do I want to be known here? And how do I more effectively accomplish that? We won't be content to merely exist—we'll want to thrive—in all that we do.

Having a purpose allows us to take more control of our personal journey. Instead of just accepting whatever experiences come our way, a purpose helps us steer away from the opportunities and experiences that don't help us become the person we want to be. It becomes a filter as we seek more fulfilling experiences and more meaningful impact.

PURPOSE MAKES HEROES

Many inspiring figures—those whose legacies have stood the test of time—were driven by purpose, and bold purpose at that. Their reasons for being ran deep and were bigger than them, which is precisely what allowed them to act with courage and have the significant impact on the world that they did.

Consider Harriet Tubman. She escaped slavery in 1849, fleeing from the slave state of Maryland to the neighboring free state of Pennsylvania. But she did not stop there. As she later said, "I was a stranger in a strange land; and my home, after all, was down in Maryland; because my father, my mother, my brothers, and sisters, and friends were there. But I was free, and they should be free."[24]

Tubman's purpose was clear—freedom for all, not just herself. She returned to the South, at great personal risk, first to free her family, then others as well. By 1860, Tubman had completed thirteen trips and helped more than seventy people escape slavery. She enabled at least fifty more to free themselves by providing detailed routes they could follow to reach sanctuary in Canada. During the Civil War, she fought for freedom by serving the Union as a nurse at Port Royal and as a scout during the Combahee River Raid.

Like Abraham Lincoln, Harriet Tubman was not some kind of superwoman. While she was incredibly strategic, she was not inhumanly gifted. Her superpower was her clarity of purpose and conviction and her unrelenting commitment to it, which is what drove her to make one courageous decision after another, creating an impact and a profile of extreme courage that is still honored more than 150 years later.

The power of purpose is the same for us as it is for these historical heroes. Purpose illuminates the path of courage and energizes us to keep walking it, no matter what. It is what we live for and the core motivation for us to do what we do. Our purpose should be bold and perhaps even scare us. Moreover, it should be about more than just ego. The converse is also true. Lack of a clear purpose creates a vacuum and leaves us exposed. Remember, as it's said, "If you don't stand for something, you will fall for anything."[25]

AN EXERCISE IN SOUL SEARCHING

You may already know what your purpose is (you may even have been tasked with writing a "statement of purpose" at some point in your life), but it could be that it's not quite clear to you yet. It certainly wasn't clear to me for many years, even though some elements of it were there, budding behind the scenes. As a child, I knew I was motivated by curiosity about the world and achieving excellence, but I didn't get an inkling of my purpose until I was in my twenties. But note that even then, I did not make it central to my life. It wasn't until my moment of awakening a few years ago that I faced the truth—I wasn't living my best life at adidas. This led to a complete reassessment of my professional life and hard internal reckoning. I decided then to make a monumental personal shift, choosing my purpose as my guiding light, which is manifest today in my fervent message about the transforming potential and power of courage in all our lives.

Sometimes, awakening happens effortlessly, we get a flash of truth, and suddenly we know without a doubt the purpose of our life. In most cases, life presents opportunities for us to reflect on our purpose—a major birthday, the passing of a loved one, or the accomplishment of a milestone. And it is up to us to seize the moment and seriously reflect on the meaning of our life.

However, in the busyness of life, it's easy to let those opportunities go by without such reflection. I certainly have. Back in 2002, as my graduation from Harvard Business School approached, a classmate started a photo project. He invited graduating students to have their portraits taken and posed the same question to each: "Tell me, what is it you plan to do with your one wild and precious life?"—a line borrowed from the Mary Oliver poem, "The Summer Day." He made headshots with each student's answer printed in the foreground of the photo and displayed them around campus during graduation week. It was a powerful exhibition.

Everyone participated in the project, everyone but me, it seemed. For whatever reason, I passed up that opportunity. Perhaps I was too busy with schoolwork; I don't recall. It was a potential moment of awakening, a chance to grapple with one of life's essential questions, but I let it slip away. Had I seized it, I might have been deeply reflective about my purpose over fifteen years earlier.

As it were, my purpose did not become fully activated until a few years ago, at the same time when I decided that *courage* would become its sharp point. Maybe, like me, you've missed a few chances in life to realize your purpose. Maybe you've been too busy. Or you've been cruising through life on autopilot, and you simply haven't had a moment of awakening. And that's okay; you can create that moment for yourself. Just like me, you'll get there…if you eventually choose to get there.

All it takes is a willingness to reflect on your life with honest curiosity—without seeking approval or affirmation from others. This is your journey to walk, and though others may help, you'll have to walk it alone.

Here are some prompts I found useful in the soul searching that led me to my purpose.

WHAT I AM PROUD OF

We all have moments we treasure that show something positive about us, about who we are or what our superpowers are. These moments tend to appear as the bullet points on our résumés, the plaques on our walls, or the mementos in our desk drawers. These moments are also loaded with insights that can guide our discovery of purpose.

I was proud to lead the first vendor management inventory initiative at Gap's Old Navy brand, a tricky supply chain project in a company that had hitherto been possessive of its core processes. I was proud of the work I did at Nike to help create the commercial strategy that enabled the company to double global revenues to over $50 billion a decade later. I was proud that VF Corporation trusted me to help turn its mature jeanswear business unit into a growth business that is now a standalone publicly traded company. I was proud of overseeing some of the Creating the New turnaround at adidas and leading the overhaul of its global operating model. I am proud of my record of taking on complex work that involves business transformation of large organizations.

When I mentored an elementary school student during my time at Morehouse, I was proud when she finally opened up and started to engage with me, something her teachers said she had struggled with. I was also proud to help the Native American employee network at Nike build the strategy for the N7 brand and craft the business model that helped it grow and donate to the communities that inspired it. I am proud whenever I receive notes from students and staff from African Leadership University with gratitude that my counsel or actions while President made a lasting impact on them. I am proud of the role I have played in helping others explore their own possibilities.

WHAT I ENJOY MOST

I'm drawn to solving difficult problems, particularly those that irk people and have resisted solutions before me. I find joy in breaking down challenges and crafting innovative answers. At the core, I come alive when exploring the new, asking "What if?" or "Why not?"

Moreover, I enjoy guiding people through these complex challenges, helping them connect dots to navigate them more easily. My passion for strategy and transformation work led me to focus on people and organizational culture as the most crucial factors of success within innovative organizations. As a result of this connection, I built a parallel skillset in education management, and I am helping a new generation of future leaders learn how to develop and apply a transformational mindset.

I get asked all the time about my "career pivot" from consumer brands to higher education. I respond that I never pivoted—I realized successful brands innovate continuously, innovation cultures are healthy cultures, and leader development has a lot to do with it. I explain that my core work never changed. Whether in corporations or classrooms, I enable transformation—it's my driving passion. This connection wasn't always clear until I realized my professional experience could serve a broader purpose.

WHAT UNSETTLES ME

The way I do this is to never close my ears or look away from stories of suffering. I try not to limit my understanding of the world to all the wonderful things going on in my own life alone. I don't spend time trying to manufacture or preserve a utopian life and a constant state of happiness. I actually worry about society's fixation on happiness. While I value happiness as much as anyone else, I am often uneasy that our tendency to filter messages from or about the world for only positive stories can blind us to important realities. When we avoid anything that unsettles us, we limit our ability to have the outrage that will conceive the opportunity for courage.

I often hear people say they avoid the media because the news is too depressing. While I understand that the constant cycle of negative news can be a drag on mental health, it's how we learn about global suffering and those who need help. When they cry, should we be tuning them out? Are their calls for help in vain—falling on deaf ears? During Sierra Leone's decade-long civil war, its citizens (including my parents and siblings) pleaded for international intervention while tens of thousands died. Thankfully, my family was not harmed. The British military's eventual involvement ended the conflict but only after years of the world looking away. Critical issues that could spark our resolve often exist beyond our secure apartments, tight networks, and comfortable echo chambers.

What this three-part exercise does is get us into the practice of intentional reflection, seeking honest feedback from ourselves, developing an "inner witness," identifying core values and beliefs, understanding our patterns, and examining our internal narratives, all of which help us to disrupt our autopilot mode.

LIVE WITHOUT REGRETS

An unfulfilled life is a life full of regrets. Fulfillment emerges from nurturing your health, deepening relationships, advancing professionally, and fostering meaningful connections. It comes from seizing opportunities for growth and positive impact—not just for yourself but for others—even through challenges. True fulfillment means living a life rich in experiences and deep connections, leaving a legacy of love, wisdom, and positive change, facing your end knowing you lived in authenticity and truth, without major regrets.

Like courage, living without regrets is a lifelong journey defined not by perfection but by continuous progress. This journey demands ruthless honesty. Don't construct fairy tales about who you *wish* to be—instead, let genuine reflection reveal who you *really* are. Like staring in the mirror, you must acknowledge the pimples and deal with them. Your purpose should be something that moves you deeply, something worth fighting for and organizing your life around. It should be compelling enough to warrant accepting risks and persisting through opposition. The path between your current reality and your aspirations is where courage proves essential. You'll navigate fears, challenges, discoveries, and change. Channel your inner Harriet Tubman—willing to risk everything for what you believe is your unique contribution to the world!

Your purpose remains an ever-present guide, always encouraging further exploration and growth, motivating you to keep striving throughout your life.

ENGAGING WITH PURPOSE

Monday, December 31, 2018, was my last day at adidas. It was a bittersweet moment—despite it being the scene of the awakening that made me change my life's direction, I enjoyed my time at the company. Still, I felt liberated.

A few weeks prior, I had launched Custament Partners to pursue my mission of helping leaders and organizations transform through courage. And it came one week before I joined African Leadership University in Mauritius as its first Executive-in-Residence. The institution, founded four years earlier, was dedicated to developing Africa's next generation of ethical leaders and entrepreneurial problem-solvers. I had been in the shoes of these young people as a teen, and I was excited to meet them and walk some of their journey with them. It felt like a capstone course—revealing what I had been trained for during the preceding years. I also knew that I wanted my family to be part of the experience, so we transitioned together from Germany to the island. It was the first time I had lived on the continent in almost thirty years. This was the first step in living out a clearer sense of purpose.

It was rediscovering my purpose that brought my life full circle, back to the continent where I had first felt that itch to explore. It was a fitting place to start the next chapter of my life…one of commitment to my purpose.

FINAL WORDS—COMMIT TO YOUR WHY

My story shows that finding and committing to your purpose isn't a onetime exercise—you may need to return to this process many times in your life. When you discover your purpose, you'll discover the missing link between previously separate parts of your life. You'll recognize a connection between something you love, a talent you have, and a way to use that talent to fix something troubling to you or the community around you. It will feel like a light has been switched on.

The key is to continually engage with your purpose and find what works for you to keep it top of mind. Challenge yourself every day to improve as you undertake the journey, to better harness your skills to benefit your purpose. Remember your courage needs your purpose as much as your purpose needs your courage.

When you finally recognize a purpose that animates you and pushes you forward *and* you commit to it, you'll join that half of people worldwide who can articulate a clear sense of purpose. You'll feel much differently about life than when you were either without a sense of purpose or making the choice to forsake a calling that beckoned to you. You'll feel a different drive. A new sense of focus and clarity. You'll feel *compelled* to act.

But that doesn't guarantee that you'll consistently act with courage. After all, committing to a purpose is just the *first* choice in living a courageous life. Next, in Chapter 3, you'll need to believe in yourself and this work you have signed up for and begin to pursue it with great intention.

A CALL TO ACTION: DRAFT HOW YOU WANT YOUR LIFE REMEMBERED

Purpose is your compass—it gives you true north when the winds of fear, doubt, and distraction blow hardest. But a compass only matters if you're willing to walk the path it points to. This means not only naming your purpose but envisioning how it will be lived out—so vividly that others could tell your story even if you weren't in the room.

THE GOAL OF THIS CALL TO ACTION

To clarify your purpose in a way that fuels courageous action today—and shapes the legacy you will leave behind. When you know how you want your life to be described, you can start making the choices that will make that description true.

HOW TO BRING IT TO LIFE

1. **Name it clearly:** Attempt writing your current purpose in one plain sentence—no jargon, no corporate-speak.
2. **Test it for courage:** Ask—Does this purpose inspire me? Does it require me to take risks? Would I choose it again if starting over?
3. **Imagine your legacy:** In one hundred words or fewer, write the future tribute you'd want to hear after you have lived your purpose. Capture values, actions, and impact—not just achievements.
4. **Spot the gaps:** Look at your past month—how many of your actions reflected this purpose?
5. **Refine it over time:** Keep your tribute visible where you can notice it every day. Revisit and update it as your purpose evolves.
6. **Choose alignment now:** Identify one concrete action this week that reflects both your stated purpose and the tribute you've drafted.

KEY ENABLERS OR CHALLENGES TO BE MINDFUL OF

- **Purpose demands clarity:** If it's fuzzy, it will fail you under pressure.
- **Beware of false fuel:** Passion alone can be exciting but fleeting; purpose endures.
- **Legacy is shaped daily:** Big moments matter less than consistent choices over time.
- **Writing reveals truth:** Putting words on paper forces precision and self-honesty.
- **Alignment requires pruning:** You may have to say no to good things to make space for the right things.
- **Expect resistance:** Your vision may unsettle others; stay the course.

You already hold the pen that writes your legacy. Keep refining your tribute, keep aligning your actions to it, and live it so fully that the story you leave behind needs no embellishment. If today clarifies your "why," let tomorrow prove it—one choice by courageous choice.

CHAPTER 3

OWN YOUR POTENTIAL

"Find the place inside yourself where nothing is impossible."
—DEEPAK CHOPRA

Twenty-two years ago, when I was attending Harvard Business School, there was an extracurricular pastime for students who wanted to leave Boston to visit a part of the world where they had a common interest. We called them *Treks*. In the spring of 2001, I joined a large group of students for a two-week *South Africa Trek*. It was my first trip back to the African continent in fifteen years. The highlight of the visit was a week in Kruger National Park. If you've ever been on an African safari, you know the badge of honor among guests is spotting all the "Big Five"—the most difficult and dangerous animals to hunt on foot in Africa. The list includes the African elephant, the leopard, the Cape buffalo, the rhinoceros, and the lion. We did see all five, but none was more memorable than the lion.

Several days into the trip, our open-top jeep rounded some bushes and came to a slow stop. Our talkative guide became more businesslike. He reached behind his seat and pulled out a rifle, then pointed to a mass of shapes in the tall grass about fifty meters away.

"Over there is a pride of lions," he whispered. "Adjust yourselves now, because we are going to get close to them, and when we do, you must stay still. Whatever you do, do *not* stand."

We got the message. This was different from other wildlife we had seen. We were going into the presence of the savanna's royal family, and we were on notice not to upset the court.

The lion is perhaps the most revered of all animals, glorified in virtually every culture. I've grown up (as we all have) with stories about the lion and never questioned the reference to the male lion as king of the jungle and the lioness as his queen. *But why is the lion so revered, and who made them king and queen?*

When we see a lion surveying its territory, we can feel its sense of confidence and ownership. It is courage in animal form. The lion simply seems to presume much about its lot. It has claimed a kingdom. It believes in its own majesty and primacy. Every action the lion takes, whether to feed its pride, protect its young, or go for a walk to the watering hole, reflects this deep-seated belief, and other animals seldom challenge it. Both its purpose and potential are its own to realize. Neither is impossible. And because the lion has established this presumption across the jungle, it gets to act on it and enjoys deference from other animals.

As humans, we don't need to attack and eat other people to show our courage. Decent people don't throw their weight around and make everyone else feel scared and small, but we can learn a lot from the lion. We must feel the same way about our potential to achieve our purpose, that it is ours by right, not something we should fritter away or allow anyone to take from us. We need to take ownership of our self-actualization—our blossoming into our human best. No one can give it to us. It must not hurt them or threaten them that we are at our best. So, when we have it, no one should take it from us. If someone tries, it's our job to take it back.

Kwame Nkrumah, former Ghanaian Prime Minister and the

father of the country's independence from Great Britain, said, "Freedom is not something that one people can bestow on another as a gift. They claim it as their own and none can keep it from them."[26]

Owning your potential is necessary for the achievement of the purpose we discussed in Chapter 2. Having a purpose starts the process, but that alone is not enough to practice courage. As important as it is to know your reason for being and commit to realizing it, it means nothing unless you wake up every day with the energy and conviction to chase that purpose down by claiming your right and your potential to do so. Of course, there will be obstacles and setbacks along the way that will sow doubt in your mind about your claim to it. It's dangerously easy to start thinking you're not good enough, it's too hard, and you'll never achieve your dreams.

Those moments call for the kind of unquestioning confidence we see in the lion—that deep sense of belief in your ability and right to pursue your purpose. We are all entitled to our highest potential. Yes, I said it—*entitled*. By entitled, I mean a purpose-based right to pursue your potential—not privilege at others' expense.

CLAIM HEALTHY ENTITLEMENT

Over the last few decades, *entitlement* has become a dirty word, synonymous with being spoiled, greedy, and lazy. It's what we call those who we feel expect success without effort or those who we believe claim greatness solely through their ancestors' achievements. It's the term some critics use to describe aid programs, implying that recipients are undeserving and lazy but expecting help. When we hear "entitled," we think of unearned benefits taken at others' expense.

But if you can look past the negative connotations, you'll realize that there are some things to which you are entitled. The early American settlers certainly believed that sentiment when they declared independence from Britain: "We hold these truths to be self-evident, that all men are created equal, that they are endowed by their Creator with certain unalienable Rights, that among these are Life, Liberty, and the pursuit of Happiness."

In the same way, Native Americans were entitled to defend and protect their homes and families from settlers when they were threatened. Enslaved carpenter and preacher Nat Turner, in Southampton County, Virginia, was entitled to seek his freedom and to resist servitude in 1831.[27] As was Simón Bolívar when he fought to liberate much of South America from Spanish rule in the 1800s. Chief Bai Bureh was entitled to fight against the imposition by colonial rulers of a Hut Tax on indigenous peoples' owned homes in Sierra Leone in 1898.[28] Malala Yousafzai was entitled to resist the Taliban's efforts to deny her and other girls their right to education in 2008. Volodymyr Zelenskyy and the Ukrainian people were entitled to fight back and protect their country from occupation and annexation by Russia in 2022. I could go on.

Freedom from oppression is something you *do* deserve, just for being alive—a thing you have a right to claim and that should come at no one else's expense. You don't have to ask permission or prove your worthiness to pursue it. Some freedoms are enshrined in the law, but others slip out of focus, to our detriment.

Like this one: *you are entitled to your own potential*!

You have the right to make the absolute most out of your life. You *deserve* to be an amazing person with a noble purpose. You're entitled to become the best person you can be. You're entitled to live a fulfilling life. Get comfortable with claiming this entitlement. It's yours, and to live a courageous life, you must believe you're worthy of it.

A VOICE IN THE DARK

Once you discover what gives your life meaning, no one should believe in it more intensely than you. Like the lion, you can't allow anyone, *not even yourself*, to deny you that. You must claim your purpose and fiercely protect it from doubt by owning your potential. This is your path to a fulfilling life. If you don't believe that this purpose is *yours* and that you *deserve* it, it will remain nothing more than a dream.

Belief is an idea until it's tested. My first test came at nineteen, in the dark of our dining room. I came remarkably close to letting a life-changing opportunity slip away one evening while in my first year at the University of Sierra Leone, still hopeful of winning a scholarship to obtain my college education in the US.

I lived in the dorms, but every Friday, I came home to pick up supplies, enjoy a home-cooked meal, and spend time with my parents and younger siblings. One evening, we had finished dinner, and I was opening mail my parents had saved for me. Due to the frequent and long power outages that were common in the city at the time, the room was dark, illuminated only by a lantern that flickered at the dining table where I sat with my siblings who were doing homework. My parents sat a few feet away, barely visible in the dim light.

I picked up an envelope, looked at the return address, then opened it eagerly. As I scanned the words on the letter inside, my excitement faded. I finished reading and tossed the note on the table with an audible groan.

"What is it?" I heard my mom's voice in the darkness.

"It's from one of the schools I applied to, Morehouse College. I was accepted but with only partial aid...so I guess I can't go," I replied. By this time, Sierra Leone was mired in economic decline, and my dream to attend college outside the country was receding fast, as there was no way my parents could afford it and no way I could enroll without substantial financial aid. I had the grades, but still, securing acceptance with a full scholarship was hard. Ridiculously hard.

There was a long silence, then a reproach from my mom.

"You need to be more confident," she counseled, "or nothing you want in life will happen."

"But—"

"You must believe. Let's work on it. We will find a way."

That is my first message here—believe.

OVERCOMING ROADBLOCKS

Those words unlocked a frenzy of activity. Once my mom had made it clear that letting the opportunity slip away was not an option, my parents sprang into action. They both took on extra jobs to earn funds to qualify me for a visa. My mom negotiated a loan from her employer to pay for my airfare. We agreed that I would find a part-time job during the school year and that my parents would keep working the jobs to cover the remaining costs.

Try as we did, we could not produce a way to pay for my costs beyond the first year. But that did not stop my parents' confidence that this was a chance that should not be squandered. During the following few weeks, our efforts, along with support from relatives who became excited about the project, began to make the Morehouse dream feel more real.

The visa process was a major hurdle, not just because we had to prove we could pay for school but also because the US Embassy in Sierra Leone rarely granted student visas. Appointments usually took months to secure and often resulted in a visa denial. A contact at the embassy advised me when to show up, and I did, clutching my college acceptance letter and other documents. A heavily armed security guard refused to let me in. But I was newly armed too—

with my mom's persistence and my own growing determination that nothing would stop me. I was not going to let the goal for which I had labored for a decade be shattered curbside at the US Embassy. I showed him the letter, pleaded with him, and refused to leave when he looked away. Eventually, he took pity on me and let me into the building. That was one major obstacle overcome. Once inside those doors, I submitted my visa application, and after a few days of nervous waiting, it was granted!

Four months later, I left Sierra Leone for the very first time to study at Morehouse College in Atlanta. I arrived in the US at the end of July 1991 clutching a small bag of belongings and twenty-five dollars tucked away safely in my pocket.

The ability to overcome obstacles is what a dogged embrace of our goals and persistence gets us. Owning our potential gets us in the game. We can't win from the sidelines. No matter how ill-prepared we feel, we need to find the courage to put ourselves out there. And once we are on the field of play, new, previously unseen opportunities arise.

EFFORT INSPIRES SUPPORT

The story of owning my potential does not end there. In fact, as you will learn, it will never end for any of us. We must keep pursuing this claim, each second of each day we live. At Morehouse, I worked relentlessly both in school and at different times selling hotdogs in a downtown Atlanta mall, cleaning tables at a fast-food chain north of the city, as a housekeeper at a midtown Atlanta hotel, and as an office assistant on campus. Every chance I got throughout my first year, I petitioned the school for more financial aid, and my anxiety rose as my first year ended. Would my worst fears be realized? Would I have to drop out of school and return home? On the last day of freshman year, I was summoned to the Office of Financial

Aid, where I received great news! I had been granted a full scholarship, including tuition, room, and board, for my remaining three years at the school.

On that dark evening sitting around our dining table with my family, I did not feel entitled to my potential. I lacked confidence. I was engaged but passively accepting roadblocks—if I wasn't good enough for a full scholarship, maybe I didn't deserve to go. Maybe it wasn't meant to be. Maybe the University of Sierra Leone—the comfortable path—was good enough, even though it didn't do much for my dream to explore and break through the barriers to the big world beyond our borders. I was ready to settle and convince myself that that was what was meant to happen.

I learned a lifelong lesson from the voice in the dark that evening—in a small moment that ultimately changed the course of my entire life. My mother pushed me to believe not only in my potential but also in my duty to catalyze opportunities for myself. On that fateful night, I started to understand obstacles as normal occurrences in every journey of consequence. I began to understand that they are not the end of the road, as I had been viewing them, but rather challenges to overcome to start a new chapter of my story. I also began to understand that there are enough obstacles out there. I don't need to make myself an additional roadblock to my own success.

I also realized that serendipity happens, but you must place yourself in its way. One form it can take is attracting people who are inspired by your story and want to help. But first I had to accept agency over the situation and organize all the resources available to me to get to where I wanted to go. I had to start believing in my ability—and my *right*—to pursue my dreams and to achieve them through my own leadership and effort. Problems and obstacles are part of the process, but problems are created to be solved. If I were not a believer in me, how could I expect others to bet on me?

FINDING CONFIDENCE

I am not the only one to battle self-doubt, and neither are you, of course. Even elite athletes must deal with self-doubt. With each new level of achievement comes a new level of competition. Once an athlete turns professional, they realize they are no longer in the minor leagues. They're now judged against the best in the country, if not the world. And it can be intimidating. It's hard for many to maintain the swagger they had on their way up. But it is not just talent but also confidence that propels athletes to reach higher levels in the first place. Self-belief is so crucial, in fact, that many sports trainers say that they'd rather give athletes a magical confidence pill than the best training regimen.[29]

Confidence is like a wonder drug. It reduces anxiety and helps people perform under pressure. It quiets the doubting voices in the back of the mind, which makes it easier to overcome adversity.

You might be asking: What if my lack of confidence is, well, justified? What if I don't have what it takes, and I'm just kidding myself with these grand ideas?

It's true; the top of any field—business, politics, sports, entertainment—is a rarefied place. Statistically, most people who aim for it don't make it all the way there. Even if we have raw talent in abundance, it still takes hard work, persistence, sacrifice, and maybe a little luck. There are no guarantees. But I am not talking about being the best in the world—I am talking about putting your best foot forward.

Peanuts creator Charles Schulz,[30] *Harry Potter* author J.K. Rowling,[31] and media personality Oprah Winfrey[32] were all written off at some point in their careers, and still, all of them, fueled by confidence in themselves, came back and proved their naysayers wrong. In fact, they each went on to create legacies that will not be easy to match.

Yet the only real difference between ambitious dreams and

delusional ones is in our awareness of reality. If we recognize the challenges ahead of us, put in the work, and pay attention to the feedback we get along the way, we are in effect playing to win. And even if we don't reach the highest peak we choose to climb, we'll get a lot farther than if we had set our sights lower.

COURAGE PILGRIM IN ACTION
ROOSEVELT GILES (CONSCIOUS CAPITALIST)

"I've never met a stranger."

Roosevelt Giles is one of the most confident and self-assured people I have met. But, if you were to meet him, no one would fault you for not appreciating that he was not destined to be so. Born the ninth of ten children, he came into the world next to a wood pile, where his pregnant mother went into labor, steps from where she had been toiling in a field in Kelton, South Carolina. As sharecroppers, his illiterate parents and their kids worked that land in near poverty until 1964, when one of his siblings bought them out of service. Nonetheless, Giles' parents had big plans for their children and taught them that they were the same as others who had more means. "What you put between your eyes," they told him, "can never be taken from you," unlike the harvested crops they were always cheated out of. Their confidence belied the fact that their kids only made it to school when it was too rainy to pick cotton. Nonetheless, this message was Roosevelt's first introduction to the concept of his potential transcending his circumstance and the power of self-worth and self-confidence to enhance his life prospects.

Before his only brother died on Thanksgiving in 2013, he made Roosevelt promise to run a marathon in all fifty states and all seven continents, ostensibly to distract him from going into depression after his brother's passing. By December 2014, Roosevelt, who had never run a marathon before the promise, completed marathon number fifty in Hawaii. And he never stopped running, even after surpassing his brother's initial challenge and despite needing four stents for a severe blockage in one of his arteries.

In truth, Roosevelt's life is a mesmerizing marathon.

For much of the early part of it, Roosevelt nursed a severe stutter, sometimes needing to stamp his foot to get the words out, at great cost to his self-esteem. He needed to fix that if he were to live up to his parents' dream, so one day he stood in front of a mirror and tried to overcome his stutter. He resolved that, rather than try to hide it, he would go out of his way to engage people and talk his way out of his condition. And he dedicated himself to that!

Today, Roosevelt is not only a successful Atlanta-based global entrepreneur and investor, but he also thrives by meeting people and putting his quiet style of self-confidence to effective use for causes he supports. He has built a massive and impressive network (a venerable Who's Who in the global corporate landscape) of purpose-driven business partners and admirers, sits on corporate boards, and is a sought-after speaker. He invokes his grandparents, parents, and family often and credits them, along with his mentor, famed South Carolina executive Roger Milliken, for the self-belief that drives him. Roosevelt is committed to "paying it forward."

Giles' years as a sharecropper indelibly shaped his life and world view. When I first met him at an event at the NASDAQ stock exchange in January 2024, Roosevelt's confidence shone bright like a beacon. In a large meeting room, a group of executives stood around and listened intently as he shared how corporate board members could help companies do good while doing well. Despite his incredible success, he remains very accessible. At heart, he's still the humble kid from Kelton with big dreams.

He takes seriously his ability to put his immense network to work on his vision to change how capitalism works and stays in close touch with the executives he has mentored along the way. I am proud to be one of them.

Asked what his superpower is, Roosevelt's answer is swift and simple, yet bold: "I am dedicated to helping to change how business is done and giving back to society, which has given me so much. I know I can't do it alone, so I must be confident about dreaming big and finding strangers to partner with, and I am never shy about approaching one. I would rather give out than give in." And so it is.

DISTINGUISHING BETWEEN DELUSION AND DISCERNMENT

Like many aspects of the courage journey, building self-belief is a delicate dance. On one hand, one could end up being delusional when what you need to be is discerning.

Suppose you believe you can inspire change through public speaking. If you pay attention while on stage, your audience will give you plenty of hints as to whether you are a great speaker.

A delusional person will take the stage with confidence but won't notice any feedback given. They won't see everyone falling asleep during their speech because a delusional person ignores reality.

A discerning person is different. She also takes the stage with confidence but is acutely aware of reality. She takes note of the jokes that didn't go over well, the inspirational quote that got a yawn, or the big finish that fell flat. Someone with discernment recognizes setbacks, then uses their confidence to hone their skills for the next challenge or the next opportunity.

The main difference between discernment and delusion, then, is self-awareness.

Barack Obama is a good example. When you see him in the present, it's hard to imagine that he ever had to nurture his self-belief. But he's only human, of course. In 2001, his confidence wavered. He had just lost a primary for a US congressional seat the year before, and a media consultant strongly discouraged him from running for statewide office. In his book, *The Audacity of Hope*, he recalls that time:

> I began to harbor doubts about the path I had chosen; I began feeling the way I imagine an actor or athlete must feel when, after years of commitment to a particular dream, after years of waiting tables between auditions or scratching out hits in the minor leagues, he realizes that he's gone just about as far as talent or fortune will take him. The dream will not happen.[33]

After defeat, Obama doubted, regrouped, and course-corrected. He made tough choices, rebuilt confidence, and ultimately became President of the United States. This is what self-awareness can do for self-confidence and what self-confidence can do for lofty ambition. When he reached the presidency, Obama was a more effective leader. His self-belief was strong because it had been tested along the way, not because he never needed it. He had to learn to identify his weaknesses, to encourage himself and conquer his inner critic. His confidence became a superpower.

As you battle moments of doubt, remember that those tests will make you stronger in the end, and more people go through them than you might think. That's why there's so much discussion about *imposter syndrome*—it's surprisingly common to feel like a fraud and question whether you deserve success, even when you already have it. You are not alone—keep working at it.

Self-belief is necessary. Carl Lewis, the American Olympics sprinter, once said, "If you don't have confidence, you'll always find a way not to win."[34] My former employer, adidas, has sounded a strong message here too. One of the brand's most iconic and long-running enduring marketing efforts has a simple yet powerful rallying cry that transcends sport and speaks to a belief in human potential—"Impossible Is Nothing."

There is a lot more to unpack about self-doubt and what drives it within us, so if this is a topic that interests you, I urge you to explore it further outside of this book. Later, in Chapter 8, we'll return to it when we discuss the difference between self-worth and self-confidence. Both are critical players on the road to courage.

NURTURING SELF-BELIEF

A healthy sense of entitlement, self-belief, and confidence is necessary to follow your purpose, but that's easier said than done. Most of us have *limiting beliefs* that get in the way, often without our even noticing. A limiting belief is a constraint we put on ourselves, an internal story about why we are not capable of doing something.

"I'm just not creative."

"I don't have the connections."

"I'm just one person—what difference can I really make?"

"I was accepted but with only partial aid...so I guess I can't go."

Often, these beliefs come from conditioning. Perhaps you were raised to stay humble or were taught to set *reasonable* goals. Perhaps your teachers encouraged you to have an easier fallback plan or suggested that you get your head out of the clouds. Perhaps your supervisors told you that you should stay with the program, that the higher-ups probably knew best. Perhaps, as a kid, grown-ups kept shushing you and saying that "children should be seen and never heard." Perhaps a vengeful date or spouse said you would never amount to much. Or perhaps society said that your purpose was simply too audacious, or if you gained a big job, it was less about your merit or hard work but more about a handout due to your race or gender.

Wherever you learned your limiting beliefs, you'll need to *unlearn* them to claim your potential. You'll need to dismantle them to practice courage. You'll need to open your mind to the idea that your life has an innate potential to blossom in extraordinary ways. Then you'll need to assure yourself that your purpose is not only possible but also *likely*. Moreover, your purpose represents your own unique gift to the world. It may be the only chance that exists to change the status quo. Your purpose *will* come to fruition through your efforts. And it will happen because *you* are exactly the right person to lead the campaign.

Building and maintaining our self-belief should be a part of our daily routines in the following ways.

DARE TO DREAM

As we saw in the previous chapter, we can't overestimate the need for constant clarity of purpose. A ton of confidence comes from just knowing what you are about. It doesn't matter if you don't know *how* you'll pursue your purpose.

By the time I was eleven, I knew I wanted to study in the United States and work on Wall Street. I also aspired to attend Harvard. I had no idea how I would make those things happen, but I kept the dream alive in my mind until, eventually, I found a way. My mom certainly knew how important it was to me, and she helped me guard the goal and not fritter it away.

Consider, also, Wangari Maathai's audacious dream: restore Kenya's degraded landscapes by putting tools in women's hands. It reframed "tree planting" as women's power and an act in democracy. She began in 1977 with a backyard nursery and a simple task—plant one tree—then built the Green Belt Movement that mobilized communities, expanded civic courage, and ultimately led to tens of millions of trees and a Nobel Peace Prize. A strong dream fuels courage because it names a future worth the friction.[35]

OBSESS OVER YOUR VISION

Earlier I mentioned that I founded a consultancy in 2019. In my strategy work, once a client has determined a vision, I challenge the leadership team to ask: once this vision is alive, what would this business look like? Then we drill down into the organization with this query until each department has curated its own image of future success. This question takes the strategy off the page and makes it a desired possibility in people's minds.

Obsessing over your goal can trigger a kind of virtuous cycle in your brain known as the Baader–Meinhof phenomenon—when you're so focused on something, you start to notice things related to it everywhere.[36] For example, once I decided to author this book, suddenly it seemed like everyone around me was writing books. It felt like each time I left the house or spoke to someone, I found arrows pointing me toward something related to book writing. I met more authors and had more conversations about book writing than I ever expected, which initiated me into a global community of writers, educated me about the process, and further built my confidence to pursue it.

The Baader–Meinhof phenomenon is also called frequency illusion. It's not that the thing just became more common—your brain has started paying more attention to it. This effect has two parts: selective attention, where your mind unconsciously looks for the thing, and confirmation bias, where each new sighting reinforces your sense that it's everywhere. The key point to take away is that nothing changed in the universe except for your sense of focus!

ASK: WHAT MUST BE TRUE?

Belief needs a blueprint. Vision becomes executable when you ask, "What must be true?"

When I was at VF Corporation, we adopted a practice not only of envisioning success but also asking ourselves "What must be true?" for that vision to be realized. Nike had a similar approach: "Plan with the end in mind." These approaches spark detailed conversations that give work plans direction and energy. They are exercises in painting potential in thoughtful dimensions and claiming success through targeting the plausible actions that are designed to make it happen.

I want to hammer home this point. In business strategy, a perennial debate rages over whether change initiatives need to be planned forward or planned back. A plan forward approach starts with where you are today and then looks forward. The risk is that the view forward is tempered by preserving the status quo and knowledge of current or past organizational limitations and therefore is never bold enough to drive meaningful change. A plan back approach (which I prefer) is supposed to challenge us to imagine a new future, then determine how to make it happen as if with a blank sheet of paper. The risk is you land in la-la-land or with an impossible task. But this does not change the fact that envisioning success is a powerful stimulator of claiming potential and the courage that it would require. I unwaveringly plan back—this approach requires and unleashes more courage.

ACTIVELY SEEK POSSIBILITY

We have a choice in how we see the world in the many situations of life we find ourselves in. Business literature calls this the abundance versus the scarcity mindset, but I want to position this in more personal terms, including how we speak and act by examining *and* versus *but*. The *and* mindset takes the status quo and seeks to make it better by connecting it with other opportunities. It allows you to focus on potential gains. The *but* mindset focuses on your limitations, looking for reasons to stop and retreat. I understood this late in life, despite seeing it play out clearly in business. Companies that focus on limitations take a defensive stance—playing *not to lose* instead of *playing to win*—and tend to rehash the failed status quo instead of evolving, which never goes well (recall the stories of the two well-known, once-successful companies Eastman Kodak and Blockbuster). The most cautious, risk-averse businesses I have worked with were the worst performers.

I was once brought into a company to advise the head of a large business, who was looking for new strategic alternatives for the business as it lagged in sales. I spent several weeks understanding the organization and started to formulate some ideas to discuss with the leader in a one-on-one conversation. All the options would result in the business growing much more than it was at the time. I stated this good news before I started to explain what the different options were. The executive interrupted just as I was talking about the sales upside, "Why might I want to do that? It's going to need investment and come with risk. Corporate is not expecting us to grow. I don't see why I should exceed their expectations." My jaw dropped. They wanted to grow. They had brought me in to help them grow. But once we were talking about growth, it was clear that he did not believe in the potential and was not owning it, and so, in effect, he was opting for the status quo.

CHALLENGE LIMITATIONS—AND STRETCH YOUR LIMITS

As it turns out, the same is true for people. Most of us do not grow up with unlimited resources in our personal lives, so we become programmed to conserve what we have and use it in small measures.

We mostly play it safe to minimize the risk of loss. I know because I have sometimes been this way. To be courageous, the opposite attitude is required. I am not saying to just go all out and bet the farm, needlessly or recklessly, but I am saying that there are more and vast possibilities out there than you already control, so believing you need to protect what you have is already inherently self-limiting and dilutes confidence. Owning your potential means claiming what you have the potential to reach that you don't have in hand yet.

There is also a difference between limitations, roadblocks in our way, and limits, the most that we can realistically do. With confidence in our effort, we can circumvent our limitations and inch closer to our limits. What I have found is that the more limitations you overcome, the higher heights you can reach and more capacity you gain—effectively allowing you to conquer old limits and strive to break past new ones.

My mom saw me as capable, and when I followed her cues, my life was forever changed. She saw my potential and owned it for me before I knew how to own it for myself. She saw my life as full of abundance. That simple difference in approach made the difference for me. I broke through the limitations and limits of the past and kept on growing!

ADOPT POSITIVE SELF-TALK

Your words matter—they often become self-fulfilling prophecies—or, as I like to put it, wherever the engine goes, the rest of the train goes. I became more aware of this as a father, when I heard my effortlessly talented kids begin to use words like "I can't" and then act on those words. If "I can't" is the promise you make to yourself, that's the promise you will keep.

As discussed earlier, athletes know this well; when you see them in TV close-ups mouthing words to themselves out on the field, they're pumping themselves up, verbally affirming what they know they can do.[37] And as sports psychologists will tell you, it really works.

As I shared above, experiment with eliminating "but" from your vocabulary. Try replacing "but" with "and" and notice the difference it has on you and the people with whom you're speaking. "I'd like to learn to play the piano, but I don't have any time" sounds innocuous enough; however, it cements your resignation and forecloses any possibility of learning the instrument. "I'd like to learn to play the piano, and once I am done with this project, I'll start lessons" keeps your goal alive and signals your intention to act.

Positive self-talk gives us a way to mentally practice how we want to be, which influences how we act, who we listen to, and ultimately, what we *become*.

ASK FOR HELP

The first day of orientation at Morehouse, the long-term Dean of Admissions, Sterling Hudson, stood in front of all the first-year students and said, "There are two words I want you to learn while you are here that could make the difference between succeeding or not graduating. They are 'Help me.'" He made us repeat the words to him and then turn to the students sitting to the right and left of us and say to them again, "Help me." Knowing how to ask for help is a simple insurance policy against risk and uncertainty, and an extra boost to confidence. The opposite is doing things alone, knowing full well that your abilities are limited and finite and remaining unsure of yourself. One of my managers used to remind us about seeking and finding solutions—even if something may be new to you, but it is certainly not new to the world; ask others for help.

To practice this act more, join a group of like-minded individuals. Groups made up of people who are committed to a similar purpose provide opportunities for growth. I am in a few accountability groups today, including some with seasoned corporate executives who are building governance careers. Each of us has doubts and needs support on occasion. This is not a sign of weakness but a quest for strength. We'll talk more about this in Chapter 5.

LET YOUR VOICE BE HEARD

As a lifelong introvert, I understand the temptation to be reticent and be more observant and reflective of what's happening around you. And while it's important to listen to others more than we speak, it's also important to practice making your own voice heard.

I learned this at Harvard Business School, which uses Socratic case discussion as its primary method of learning. Grades were largely based on real-time participation in the discussion of the case at hand in each class, and during the first few weeks, I was slow to jump into the conversation. Quickly, I found myself struggling in many of my classes because of my reluctance to speak up. Even worse, the more the semester progressed, the harder it felt to get into the fray. As a result, my confidence started waning. It took urgent warnings from some faculty and coaching from an advisor to force me to put my anxieties aside and get in the game.

I had to learn some tricks, like preparing talking points beforehand, speaking early in the class period, and learning that asking a probing question was as helpful as asserting a point. But once I took the plunge, everything changed. It's one of the best lessons of my business school experience: growing confidence by making your voice heard and doing so early, frequently, and assertively. You must build the habit of creating your own space and occupying it with confidence. If your voice is not heard, you become invisible. Others will talk around, above, and through you. Later, they might not even remember that you were there.

This does not imply that you must speak without thinking or begin dominating conversations, both of which run counter to our definition of courage as thoughtful and not self-serving or rash. There is a difference.

CELEBRATING SMALL WINS

We don't build confidence only by thinking positively about our aspirations; we also build it by acknowledging the wins we've already tallied. They reinforce our sense of accomplishment and belief in ourselves and motivate us to take the next step.

Helga Hengge, the mountaineer and motivational speaker, spoke at adidas while I was an executive there. She shared that when she was climbing Mount Everest, it was important to stop every so often, look back, and see how far she'd come.[38] A reminder of the incredible distance she'd already conquered made the way forward seem less intimidating. Every boost to her confidence mattered, and that was always a strong one.

We generally assume that celebrations sequentially follow the completion of a task, but who said it must be so? Celebrating small milestones mid-task are just as valid and perhaps even more valuable in filling our emotional gas tanks to keep plodding ahead. As long as it helps, do it!

I know we are all inherently self-critical, but that's even more reason to believe the business of building courage needs all the help it can get. We'll talk about fear and failure in the coming chapters and how they can play a role in limiting your courage. The reality is that there are many factors already lined up against you, so don't focus only on the things you did not do well. Be a cheerleader for yourself. Celebrate all the wins you make—on this journey, they are much more important to acknowledge.

FINAL WORDS—OWN IT. THEN ACT.

You already know your purpose. It's time to stop questioning it and bring it to life. It's no one else's job but your own.

It's time to be the lion.

Like the lion who moves through the savanna certain of his dominion, find that place inside yourself where nothing is impossible—and claim it as your own.

Owning your potential begins with a choice. You can choose to embody self-doubt—shrinking back, questioning your place, and staying silent. Or you can choose to believe in yourself, step forward with confidence, and claim the life you are meant to live. One choice limits you; the other expands you.

Purpose gives you the "what" and the "why." Potential is the next rung on the ladder of growth. Self-belief is the "how"—the bridge that carries you from where you are now to the future you seek. Without it, purpose remains an idea. With it, purpose becomes action.

Believing in your potential means daring to get in the game, taking your shots, and playing to win. It means cheering for yourself while drawing strength from those who support you. It means asking for help when needed and celebrating progress along the way.

And it means facing fear head-on. Nervousness, anxiety, and doubt are not signs of weakness but evidence that you are growing. Courage is not the absence of these feelings—it is the choice to act despite them. The wrong choice is self-doubt.

You've learned how to claim your potential; next, in Chapter 4, we'll unmask the fear that tries to take it back.

A CALL TO ACTION: CHALLENGE YOUR SELF-LIMITING BELIEFS

Courage cannot be outsourced. It cannot be delegated, inherited, or built for you by someone else. It is a force that must emanate from within—a journey you own entirely and are fully accountable for. Owning your potential is both a personal right and a nonnegotiable obligation you owe yourself. And that means refusing to let others disempower you—or to disempower yourself.

THE GOAL OF THIS CALL TO ACTION

To consciously dismantle the self-imposed barriers that keep you from living and leading courageously, replacing them with truth, evidence, and a bias toward action.

HOW TO BRING IT TO LIFE

1. **Identify the belief:** Name one self-limiting belief you return to often. Write it plainly in your journal.
2. **Interrogate it:** Ask—is this truly an obstacle, or am I conjuring it up?
3. **Gather the evidence:** List what supports the belief and what contradicts it—especially moments where you've surprised yourself in the past.
4. **Reframe the script:** Change "I can't" to "What steps can I take to make this possible?"
5. **Act on the new frame:** Take one small, deliberate risk this week that directly challenges the old belief.
6. **Celebrate the win:** Recognize the courage it took, no matter what the size of the result.

KEY ENABLERS OR CHALLENGES TO BE MINDFUL OF

- **Past success is proof:** You've overcome doubt before—you can again.
- **Bias toward growth:** Favor the evidence that builds your confidence and forward motion.
- **Risk fuels courage:** Betting on yourself often pays off.
- **The biggest barrier is you:** Moving beyond self-limiting beliefs starts with getting out of your own way.
- **Don't be delusional:** Balance and navigate feedback with honesty and lots of self-awareness.

You've surprised yourself before—do it again. Break your own ceilings, refuse to be the one holding yourself back, and watch how quickly your courage expands into every part of your life.

CHAPTER 4

UNMASK FEAR

"Courage is not the absence of fear, but rather the assessment that something else is more important than fear."

—FRANKLIN DELANO ROOSEVELT

In the late afternoon of March 16, 2020, I went for a short walk around the grounds of African Leadership College in Mauritius, the maiden campus of African Leadership University. This was my favorite time of the day when at the school—the students were the most relaxed, having finished classes and ready to enjoy dinner. As usual, the grounds were buzzing with activity—students were lounging in the grand hall, jogging along the long tree-lined driveway, playing basketball on the outdoor courts, and sitting in the central courtyard. To the west, the sun was sinking in a magnificent array of colors.

It was a perfect scene—Africa's bright future against the backdrop of Africa's incredible beauty. On any other day, the scene would have brought me peace, and I would have paused to take it all in. But on this day, it tied knots in my stomach as I continued my walk without stopping. As President of the university, I was about to make the biggest decision of my tenure, and one that would shatter the beautiful and tranquil picture and significantly impact the lives of the unsuspecting students...and I was afraid.

The COVID-19 virus had been in the global news for a few months, and since the start of that year, my leadership team had watched its progress with growing apprehension. We had already stepped-up hand sanitization and limited visitors to our campuses, even while there were no recorded cases of the virus on the island of Mauritius and very few in Rwanda, the location of our sister campus. Beyond that, we had not raised an alarm with the students and staff, even though my team was monitoring the pandemic's progression closely. Infections and fatalities continued to rise all around the world, including in other African countries. Although we knew little about the disease or how to treat it successfully, it was believed at the time that life-saving treatment involved ventilators, and the word was that there were precious few on the island.

I had just left an all-day meeting of the full university management team, where we had spent hours discussing the risks and what-ifs. Our conclusions had focused on not *if* but *when* the pandemic would reach the island or proliferate in Kigali, in Rwanda. Many unanswered questions plagued us: In Mauritius' complex demographic mix, how would our students (almost all foreign nationals) access limited COVID-19 medical care? And in Rwanda, where our nonresidential campus held twice as many students scattered across Kigali, how could we track them and assure their parents of their well-being? If any students were admitted to hospital, would we be able to be by their side or advocate for them?

The questions kept coming. Would the students be safer living and studying on the campuses or at home? If either government ordered a lockdown, could we keep the essential services running? How would government officials react if our lockdown were premature when they were trying to allay mass panic? How would we continue to deliver education in all the scenarios we considered? What would sending students home and investing in digital delivery mean for our already cash-strapped finances and for our ability to keep the lights on during this unprecedented global catastrophe? Could the institution survive?

There were no perfect choices. Each unanswered question raised the level of uncertainty about what the future held, and with it my level of fear. If we didn't shut down the campus, we might be setting the stage for a tragic loss of life. If we did, the powerful work of this one-of-a-kind university would be disrupted, and we might be sending some students home to even higher-risk circumstances, from which the university had been a refuge.

A decision was needed. It was my responsibility as President. My fear could not stand in the way of doing my job, especially when the welfare of over two thousand students was at stake.

That wasn't the first time I felt gripped by fear, and it certainly wouldn't be the last. Fear is natural—and often a signal that courage is required.

RECOGNIZING FEAR AS A SIGNAL

Tens of thousands of years ago, long before video doorbells and spam blockers, we had built-in alarm systems that alerted us to threats. Innate, biological warning signals have been wired into us. Of course, back then, the dangers weren't porch pirates stealing our Amazon deliveries or hackers breaking into our inbox. The threats were more immediate—saber-toothed cats that wanted to eat us, for example. So we needed those biological instincts telling us when to run and how to survive.

Saber-toothed felines have been extinct for ten thousand years, but our innate warning system is still with us because, well, they aren't the only things that can harm us. When your brain spots a possible threat, the amygdala—small clusters of neurons deep in each temporal lobe—sounds the alarm and signals the hypothalamus. That flips switches on two stress systems. First comes the fast track (the "fight-or-flight" response): adrenaline surges, your heart pounds, and your blood pressure and breathing jump. Then, the slower backup (the HPA axis) releases cortisol over minutes to keep you on alert. The amygdala doesn't work alone—areas like the hippocampus and prefrontal cortex help judge the situation—but together they prime the body to fight, flee, or freeze.[39] Technical jargon, yes, but the point I make is that when you start feeling all these sensations, *there is nothing wrong with you*—this is just the body doing its thing.

While this mechanism kept us alive in prehistoric times, and still does in times of perceived danger, now it also often hampers our ability to function in modern society. Our warning bells go off before giving a presentation. They go off before asking someone on a date. They go off before a job interview. Surely, you have found yourself in one or more of these situations before. Maybe your hands were shaking, you started sweating, or you felt sick to your stomach. But let's take a step back and think outside of those emotions and feelings.

Why does the survival alarm go off before an interview?

No one has ever been eaten in a job interview.

The problem is that our warning bells are triggered in all types of situations from the serious to the mundane. It's as if we're playing a new game but still running the old software. Our instincts haven't adapted to the largely predator-less world in which we now live. If you tried to avoid every little thing that pings your amygdala, you'd probably never leave the house—forget about living a courageous life.

I don't want to make light of fear and risk—both are real, and both are extremely important in our lives as humans. However, we tend to make them larger and scarier—and therefore, more consequential to our lives than we should. To be courageous, we don't need to ignore fear (please don't take that as my message). Rather, we need to engage fear more deeply and challenge it when it shows up and tries to stop us in our tracks.

Let's start with just one small mental tweak—our fear response isn't a *warning*—it's a *signal*. It doesn't mean danger is ahead. It just means our brain is predicting possible discomfort...and that prediction may or may not be correct. And even if you do experience discomfort, it will not necessarily be debilitating or life ending.

CHALLENGING YOUR FEAR RESPONSE

Before you take your fear too seriously, it's important to understand that this signal system suffers from three major flaws.

CONFLATING DISCOMFORT WITH DANGER

The first issue with our natural signal system is that discomfort can include plenty of things that don't qualify as danger, and yet our system doesn't distinguish between them. Discomfort triggers a fear reaction that's often just as alarming as the fear triggered by real danger. For example, *uncertainty* can be uncomfortable. When we have no idea what the result of an endeavor will be, we feel discomfort, and that drives us to stick with what we know. *Attention* can also trigger fear. We feel uncomfortable being in the limelight because we don't want to fail publicly, which we think might bring a social cost. We feel uneasy with *change*. When we are confronted with an unfamiliar environment and forced to learn new skills, we're worried that we won't be able to learn fast enough to succeed. We're also uncomfortable with *sacrifice*. We worry about experiencing pain, struggling, or giving up something we cherish and having to adjust to a new way of living.

This conflation of discomfort with danger explains why we may feel terrified about speaking up at a school board meeting. Speaking brings uncertainty and public attention but has never killed anyone outright. On the other hand, the same person can be completely comfortable whizzing down a freeway at one hundred miles per hour. We need to ask ourselves which is more dangerous. While driving on the freeway is a well-documented hazard, there are probably zero deaths from TED Talk. But speeding along in a car is familiar, private, routine, and easy, so it doesn't trigger a fear response. Giving a presentation, on the other hand, is *uncertain* (we don't know how it will be received), brings *attention* (if we fail, we fail publicly), is a *change* from our normal routines, and requires *sacrifice* (a lot of work to prepare).

Also, when it comes to predicting discomfort, our minds exaggerate possible negative outcomes and overblow their likelihood. Psychologists describe a "negativity bias": we attend more strongly to losses and adverse signals than to gains, and we are hard-wired to assume and prepare for the worst. This natural inclination toward pessimism is all biology, and fear thrives on it!

PROJECTING LEARNED BIASES

The second problem with our fear response is that our presumptions and expectations are sometimes biased. As we go through life, we accumulate all kinds of ideas about what's comfortable and what's not, some based on firsthand experience and many others based on stories, observations, or pure imagination. This is unconscious bias—automatic mental shortcuts we use to judge people or situations, often without realizing it. These biases are shaped by our background, experiences, culture, and societal norms.

The worst part is that most of the time, we're not even aware of these ideas; they lurk below the level of conscious thought, influencing us without our knowing it. For example, suppose we're trying to choose between two restaurants and ask someone for a recommendation. They (unhelpfully) respond that they like both restaurant A and restaurant B. Then, they casually add that restaurant A is in a nicer neighborhood. We might immediately become fearful of going to restaurant B and choose A instead. Based on what evidence? We're not rejecting restaurant B because the food or service received a disparaging review from a friend; we're simply allowing our fear instincts to go into overdrive just because it was suggested that restaurant A is in a "nicer neighborhood" even though nothing negative was said about restaurant B's cuisine, cleanliness, or location.

I encounter people every day who purport to know much about the African continent, but when they speak, it is to spew negative impressions. And worse, they never actually visited or even considered visiting an African country. Why? Well, in movies, books, and a myriad other ways, over the centuries a masterful job has been done depicting the continent in unflattering and scary terms—at odds with the truth or the actual experience of being there.

If we were to pay close attention, we would find that our daily decision-making is packed with unconscious bias. It makes us feel comfortable with our decisions, but that is eons removed from saying that it allows us to make the best, or even good, decisions.

FEAR CAN BE COSTLY OR INEFFICIENT

Not only are our fears misplaced, overblown, or biased, but a third problem with our fear response is that it can be costly, impacting how we make everyday spending decisions. One easy reference to make here is the insurance industry—global insurance premiums reached $7 trillion in 2024, up 8.6 percent from 2023.[40]

I recently completed a multi-week experience hike across northern Spain for which I had to pack and carry a backpack with all my necessities for the duration of the trail (about four hundred kilometers). The recommended weight for a pack is ten kilograms (about twenty-two pounds), but my first attempt at packing weighed twice as much. I had convinced myself that I needed all the items in the bag. The truth is that fear of the unknown made me entertain a slew of outlandish scenarios to be prepared for, and with each item (representing my ample collection of both rational and unfounded fears) my pack got bigger and heavier. In this case, the cost of letting fear drive me was spending money on more than I needed and, once the walk was underway, developing acute back and hip pain that threatened to derail the entire experience, had I not lightened my load midway. As my older brother, who was my walking companion, put it: "You carry your fears on your back. Let them go and walk lighter."

Yes, there is physical, psychological, and not just a financial cost to carrying fear around. This potentially gets us into lots of conversations about how we live our lives today and can improve them in the future, but suffice it to say for now that fear can be costly.

REALITY BEARS OUT DIFFERENTLY

The worst rarely happens, and if it does, it often doesn't feel as bad as we imagined it would. Lots of bad storms hit the coast of Florida each year, for example, but many are not as horrific as the nonstop news cycle makes them out to be. Fear can be potent, paralyzing, and debilitating, which is why it can easily be manipulated. Politicians campaign by invoking fear all the time. Most times, their worst pronouncements about their opponents or scary scenarios happen quite differently.

Fear and bias can also be harmful and hurtful. For example, today in the US there is increasing stigmatization of diversity initiatives.[41] These programs are cast as inherently unfair and labeled reverse discrimination. At the same time, the racial wealth gap has continued to widen, with the difference between median White and Black household wealth increasing by $49,950 from 2019 to 2022, reaching a total gap of $240,120.[42] At the same time, research by the Federal Reserve Bank of San Francisco estimates racial and ethnic gaps in economic opportunity have cost the US $51 trillion over the last thirty years.[43] The facts don't validate the fear.

These examples show what happens when the flaws in our fear-signaling system, especially regarding perceived and real risk, get magnified. It's clear that we can't blindly trust these signals. Just because you feel a sensation of fear doesn't mean there's any real danger ahead. Most likely, your mind is signaling possible discomfort, not danger, and that discomfort probably isn't as likely or as bad as you imagine it to be. If you blindly follow those signals, you're bound to make flawed decisions and miss good opportunities over your lifetime.

We shouldn't ignore those signals either, though. They're telling us something important. In fact, what you perceive as scary is often precisely what you *need*—to learn, to grow, to make progress toward your life's purpose. The sensation of fear is simply a clue that the path ahead requires courage. The sensation of fear could in fact suggest an opportunity!

So, if we can't trust or ignore our fear signals, what can we do? We can stop and examine them.

EXAMINING FEAR

Extreme fears (anxieties or phobias) that go unchecked and take control of our decisions can lower our quality of life. But the everyday fears that most of us encounter can be managed.

The key to countering fear is to examine it. We name our fear, analyze the unconscious sources, and ask ourselves if the goal on the other side is important enough to push through discomfort.

That's what I did back in Mauritius in March of 2020. At first, it seemed like every option was equally bad. Every path seemed to lead to an unfortunate outcome. But I could not hide from the decision that needed to be made. When I examined my fears more closely, I quickly realized that it was the enormity of the decision and the burden of making it without conclusive information one way or the other—the uncertainty—that scared me. What if I was wrong? How would I face our students and their parents? Would I lose credibility with the university community?

But something else revealed itself. Regardless of my own concerns about disrupting people's routines and the beautiful experience that was the university, safety was far more important. We could not and would not lose anyone to the pandemic. This would be our number one goal. I could live with disappointed students and angry parents if we shut down prematurely or unnecessarily. But if we didn't shut down and even one member of our community lost their life as a result…I couldn't live with that. I would ground my decision in the commitment that we would not risk lives, and if I turned out to be wrong, so be it.

So we took the leap and sent everyone home. The reactions were passionate and varied.

It turned out to be the right decision; just as the last students were arriving home after a hasty but orderly forty-eight-hour evacuation, the government of Mauritius announced an outbreak of COVID-19.[44] The nation locked down, banning all travel and public gatherings, including those relating to educational institutions. Rwanda shut down a few days later.[45] Had I allowed fear to paralyze me for even one more day, our students would have been stuck in limbo, unable to stay on campus or go home, struggling to access essential daily campus services, or, much worse, possibly exposed to the virus.

When I feel fear, I find it helpful to examine it by working through the following steps.

STEP 1: NAME THE FEAR

What exactly is the negative outcome you're expecting? Sometimes, simply naming the fear makes you realize how ridiculous it is. Or if it's a legitimate fear, it helps you see more clearly whether the negative outcome is something with which you could live. I can't count how many times in my life the fear was just about being *wrong* and the assumed consequential bruise to my ego. Over time, I grew to see being wrong as nothing to be ashamed of.

STEP 2: IDENTIFY ITS SOURCE

The feeling of fear can be potent but is its source as credible? Is the fear just based on a feeling you have or something someone said—and if so, who? Are they the person you would trust with something else that was important to you, such as medical advice or where to send your kids to school. Is the fear based on facts—if so, from where? Again, is the source credible? Is the messenger objective? Many of my fears have collapsed under this scrutiny.

STEP 3: ESTIMATE ITS LIKELIHOOD

As shared earlier, research has repeatedly shown that the human mind gives more weight to losses than gains—we feel them more, remember them more vividly, and overestimate their likelihood. So it helps to put a probability on the negative outcome you're anticipating, ideally one based on evidence, not just your gut feelings. You'll probably find that the chance of a bad outcome is much lower than you first thought. Many people are afraid of the dark, but how many documented cases are there of the dark attacking someone? None.

STEP 4: VISUALIZE THE BEST CASE

What if everything goes right? What do you stand to gain? What would this outcome mean for you, a goal that you have, a cause that you believe in, or the people you care about? This is why we started this book with a conversation about purpose and what motivates us. Don't simply answer these questions; imagine your dream in as much detail as possible. Visualize exactly how it will happen and how you'll feel when it does. Visualization is a powerful tool for calming your fear, boosting your confidence, and focusing your mind. Many times, our desire to achieve something meaningful is far greater than our fear of failing.

STEP 5: IMAGINE RETREATING

This is the antonym consideration to the point above. What if you run from this fear and choose the comfortable path or popular decision over the courageous one? What would you gain in the short-term, and would that gain sustain? What would you be giving up? Who would you let down? Would you regret it later? What would this say about you and what you believe in? These questions help you realize that retreating from fear isn't a neutral choice—it comes with its own risks, consequences, and implications.

I want to share one very personal experience to illustrate all the previous points.

THE NIGHT I CHOSE COURAGE

In June 1997, I was attending a friend's graduation ceremony at Dartmouth College, but I was distracted by something else happening thousands of miles away. Sierra Leone was amid a brutal civil war, and the capital city Freetown had been breached by a rebel force. Unthinkable atrocities were being committed randomly on civilians—and my parents and siblings were in a state of constant worry. Late that night, I called home with a radical suggestion—flee the country. The catch was that there were no reliable ways to do so. The airport had been closed for several months. Rebels surrounded the city. Fishermen and profiteers were loading people onto cargo boats and ferrying them to neighboring countries, where many ended up in unsanitary and unsafe refugee camps. My family had been lying low, until now. "Flee the country in one of the boats," I urged. I found out one would leave within hours for The Gambia, a small country north of Sierra Leone. Was I afraid even as I confidently urged my family to leave? I was petrified.

How did I get to such a confident, though fretful, decision?

I was sending my most beloved people into potentially more risk and more uncertainty. They were at risk at home, yes, but they had survived so far, albeit with bleaker prospects ahead. Risk at sea was different—none of them were swimmers. A few refugee boats had capsized in the weeks before. Life in a refugee camp could be horrendous too. Were something bad to happen to them, I would have to live with my role in a bad outcome for the rest of my life.

Like my predicament at ALU, every option seemed equally bad. On the one hand, they could stay at home where there was a real possibility of becoming a victim of war. On the other hand, they could flee and risk disaster at sea or relocation to a refugee camp with poor living conditions.

Boiling the quandary down to two questions, I became more confident. What was the worst outcome that could happen if they stayed behind? What was the best thing that could happen if they left home, even with all the risks? I had my answer.

A few hours before my mom and siblings (my dad decided to stay behind) left the house, we discussed how to limit risk: "Leave the home and walk casually. Take nothing with you so as not to draw unwanted attention. Keep your passports and money secure. If the boats seem too unsafe, return home. Don't worry about what happens at the destination. We are making plans for you in The Gambia."

I got off the phone and sat in the dark, the sound of their voices and goodbyes echoing in my head. They trusted me infinitely. I prayed that I would hear those voices again soon. The weight of the moment set in, and as I stared out the window into the New Hampshire woods outside, I broke down and cried.

On their part, my mom and younger siblings demonstrated tremendous courage on that day. They traveled across militarized areas to a pier on the other side of town, where they boarded a rickety vessel that was loaded with three times as many people as was safe. The voyage took twice as long as normal, leaving me a nervous wreck for nearly a week in a Lower Manhattan skyscraper where I worked at Lehman Brothers.

Conditions on the vessel were uncomfortable and unhygienic for the refugees sleeping hungry and seasick on the deck. At least one elderly passenger succumbed. My family finally arrived in The Gambia, where they were processed as refugees but spared deployment to a camp because a family friend who lived in the country stepped in to host them. They lived in his house for a year before they were selectively vetted by the US State Department and invited to resettle in the US, where they have lived since. Yes—happy conclusion, but tons of fear each step of the way!

Hopefully, this example helps you understand *how* to face fear instead of doing everything you can to avoid it or allowing it to drive your decisions. Following a thought process like this will dampen the intensity of your fear and make it easier to take courageous action. The fear might still be there, and that's okay.

Move forward anyway.

COURAGE PILGRIM IN ACTION
FRED SWANIKER (SERIAL ENTREPRENEUR)

"What's the worst that could happen?"

The sprawling portfolio of African Leadership Group (ALG) is an enviable collection of Big Hairy Audacious Goals (BHAGs).

First, in 2008, African Leadership Academy (ALA) was launched in Johannesburg, South Africa. ALA is a globally respected college prep school. African Leadership University (ALU), dubbed by some as "the Harvard of Africa," launched in Mauritius as African Leadership College (ALC) in 2015 before it expanded to Rwanda in 2017, and it is matching the student outcomes of higher education institutions in the West that are over a century older. Then there's ALx, an on-demand professional development program for tech careers founded in 2019, which generates over two hundred thousand learners each year. Most recently, Sand Technologies—an enterprise AI solutions company, which wants to help build Africa's IT sector and develop its next generation of innovators—is a separate, related, and similarly ambitious sister venture to the group. ALG has become known and respected around the world as one of the most consequential players in education innovation and human capital development on the African continent—with a simple and daring mission: to develop at least three million ethical, entrepreneurial, and empowered African leaders by 2035.

The group's founder is Fred Swaniker, a Ghanaian entrepreneur born of middle-class civil servants and who graduated from Stanford Business

School with a mission to transform the African continent before it becomes most of the global population in 2050.

Fred has been lauded around the globe for his efforts. He was recognized as a TED Fellow and a World Economic Forum Young Global Leader. He has received three honorary doctorates and was named by *Time Magazine* as one of the "100 Most Influential People in the World." He earned all these accolades, he would say, by "doing hard things."

Fred's desire to see Africa transform runs deep into his core and propels him to dream the impossible. He particularly relishes "goals that are so big that they will outlast me," and once one venture is up and running, he steps aside to let someone else run it so he can start the next one. Fred is a grandmaster at unmasking fear and has jumped repeatedly into scary landscapes and burst forth from them with world-class institutions driving breathtaking outcomes.

He still sees himself as a loquacious and inquisitive little boy from Ghana who has defied the odds to pursue big goals. He attributes his successes to his parents and teachers, who believed in his abilities and continually told him that he was destined to do something great. These affirmations fueled his confidence and ability to engage with fear.

Asked what role fear had played in his ambitions, he replied, "I am afraid all the time." Fear has been his companion from the start, but Swaniker still asserts that "most people overestimate the cost of failure." He recounts one experience while raising money to launch the academy in Johannesburg. He was dead broke, having quit his job at the blue-chip consulting firm McKinsey, sleeping on friends' couches at night, and hunting for donor dollars by day. One day after a late and unsuccessful meeting with a potential donor in New Jersey, Fred realized that he had no money to get back to his crash pad in Manhattan. He looked across the Hudson River at the bright lights in the skyscrapers, pictured some of his MBA classmates at work, and hit a psychological low. "Here I am, a Stanford MBA, and I cannot afford meals or train fare home," he recalled. As he always does, Fred placed his moment of envy in the bigger context of his work—impacting a generation of young people—and his self-pity disappeared. What if he failed? What was the worst thing that could happen? He could do what all his classmates across the river were already doing. He could go back and work for McKinsey. This was a powerful realization. He could be afraid and quit, or he could pursue his goals and perhaps fail. And the worst outcome of failure would be to rejoin one of the most coveted consulting firms in the world. Swaniker lives with fear every day, but he has always found a way to manage it and carries on pursuing BHAGs.

FEAR ERODES A GROWTH MINDSET

I have talked about the university I was honored to lead and its mission to transform an entire generation of global leaders. Its motto is "Do Hard Things," evocative of the need for leaders to be comfortable doing uncomfortable, or scary, things. Obviously, the primary goal of educational institutions such as the African Leadership University is to bring about growth in human capacity. Embracing growth, or the growth mindset, is a process, one that takes effort and one that we inculcated in all our students from their first day on campus.

The starting point for most of us is our *comfort zone*, the place where we feel the safest and most secure. However, growth demands that we move beyond this familiar territory into a space where we lack knowledge, experience, or familiarity. A lot is riding on this *new zone of learning*. It is where we deal with new challenges and, as we overcome them, convert them into new skills. However, crossing into the learning zone means a confrontation with fear.[46]

Earlier in the chapter we talked about how fear masquerades as discomfort—and brings feelings like *uncertainty, a sense of exposure, anxiety about change, need for investment, and worrying about sacrifice*. Fear's goal is for us to retreat to the comfort zone and away from growth that follows the experience of new learning and new skills acquisition. If fear always had its way, we would never leave the comfort zone. Imagine that!

It's normal to be afraid. We all feel fear. And it is normal to respond by wanting to stay in our comfort zone. This is a choice you could make but one I discourage. Our learning and growth will be slow, and courage will be elusive if fear gets to speak first and have the last say. That's because fear will bring its friends—denial, avoidance, procrastination, and excuses, all which dictate our response and crowd out courage. Together, they keep us stagnant and prevent us from growing.

To reach the growth zone, we must train ourselves to navigate through these stages. As we practice courage and consistently test our boundaries, our comfort zone gradually expands to include our learning zone. As we become accustomed to the process of growth, the pursuit of new fears and skills becomes a perpetual cycle. Our growth zone continuously evolves, just as we do.

Before any of these transformations can occur, though, we must first push through our fears. Once we respond to them appropriately, we can learn, adapt, and grow. This cyclical process of confronting fear, acquiring knowledge, and expanding our comfort zone is the essence of practicing courage.

MANAGE FEAR LIKE YOU MANAGE RISK

I find it helpful to think about our response to fear the same way businesses think about risk. Risk isn't inherently good or bad. Low risks generally come with low rewards; high risks offer the possibility of higher rewards.

Ambitious investors and entrepreneurs don't respond to high risks by shying away. They know those risks are necessary to get the extraordinary outcomes they want. So they analyze their options carefully, and when they find a substantial risk worth taking, they manage it and make the move anyway.

Today, as a board member and executive consultant, I spend much of my time advising organizations about how to pursue opportunities while mitigating risks, not running away from opportunities. Risk mitigation is essential; it shouldn't preclude opportunity. It is the same with fear. Risk and fear can make your decisions more reasoned if you learn to work with them instead of letting them steer. As you examine fear, don't just identify and catalog the threats it highlights but seek to understand them and mitigate them.

Fear, just like risk, can be analyzed and managed—and when you respond to it with true understanding, the reward will be immense. This may seem counterintuitive when our first instinct is to avoid it. But if you do that, you'll never find the source of your fear and determine whether you should run away from, or toward, it. If you make a habit of doing that, you will never learn how to find courage. That's why our response to fear is not about overcoming, controlling, or eliminating it. It's about practicing courage by looking closely at your fear and then determining an appropriate response that is based in logic.

You were afraid before you made a decision yesterday, the day before that, last week, and ten years ago...and *you're still here*.

So fear isn't the end of the world, nor is it always the risk and discomfort that it signals.

Feeling anxious or afraid is a sign that the situation you're facing is important to you and that you care about the outcome. That's a good thing. It isn't a signal for you to retreat.

Remember, fear does not play the same role today as it did for our prehistoric ancestors. Often it is reacting to and signaling more mundane risks for which we have inaccurately attributed fear. And perhaps the biggest risk that fear cautions us against is failure, which we turn to in Chapter 7. However, the true failure is allowing fear to steer you away from the courageous acts that your fulfilling life demands of you.

WHEN FEAR COMES FROM "GOOD INTENTIONS"

Just a few weeks before I graduated from college and started my first job as an investment banking analyst at Lehman Brothers, I received an invitation to dinner one Sunday. When I arrived in the ornate private dining room at a glitzy downtown Atlanta hotel, I was greeted by our host, a senior Wall Street banker, a portly gentleman dressed in an elegant three-piece suit. He had been an active recruiter and a frequent visitor to the school and had assembled a handful of graduates who, like me, were headed to New York to start new jobs on The Street. We enjoyed a sumptuous dinner, already feeling at home with the high-flying life that was ahead of us and looking forward to his after-dinner pep talk—the main reason for the event.

His opening words were full of cheer and well wishes, while the rest of his message was anything but. He reminded us that we were the chosen few and that was a responsibility never to take lightly. Then he told us bluntly no matter what we did in New York, we should not "fuck up" the opportunity for others or embarrass recruiters like him. Wall Street is brutal, he said, and many before us who had not appreciated this quickly enough had died a gruesome death on its pavements. He glowered around the table as he spoke, heaving, and when he stopped to catch his breath, his glares would often rest on the two white-eyed students who were joining his firm (thankfully, I was not one of them).

I remember his final words right before dessert was served. "When you start screwing up, you might get a few warnings. But ultimately you will run out of chances, and the last thing you will remember before you die is lying at the bottom of a grave with your colleagues shoveling dirt down on you. And if you look up, you will see me, your 'friend,' shoveling dirt on you along with them."

We were all immediately promising ourselves that we would not screw up—and maybe clenching up a little and deciding not to take many risks. Being buried alive sounded horrendous and fearsome, and what kind of people did that anyway? It was not the best way for us to regard the place where some of us hoped we would build long careers. He was well-meaning, but in retrospect, he was clearly dealing with his own fears and passing them on to us.

FINAL WORDS—LET FEAR SPEAK BUT PURPOSE DECIDE

Fear will always be present in the moments that matter most. It arrives when the stakes are high, when the next step feels uncertain, and when growth demands that you leave the safety of what you know. The wrong choice is to allow apprehension to rule, to let fear dictate your movements and keep you stuck in hesitation. That choice shrinks your world and silences your potential.

But there is another way. When you unmask fear, you begin to see it not as a stop sign but as a signal. Fear is simply an indicator that you are moving into unfamiliar territory—the very place where learning, impact, and transformation occur. Acknowledging it allows you to strip it of its power. Instead of controlling you, fear becomes a teacher, sharpening your focus and reminding you that you are alive, engaged, and stepping toward growth.

Courage does not require eliminating fear; it requires walking alongside it. Each time you choose to act in the presence of fear, you strengthen your ability to live intentionally and to pursue purpose despite risk. That choice expands you, empowers you, and builds resilience for the journey ahead.

And while unmasking your own fear is essential, there is another challenge waiting. Sometimes fear does not come from within but from the voices of others—doubts, warnings, or limitations they try to hand you. The next step in *C.O.U.R.A.G.E.* is learning to recognize and reject those distracting voices. We'll now cover this in Chapter 5.

A CALL TO ACTION: MAKE FEAR A DECISION-MAKING PREREQUISITE

Fear isn't a red light—it's a flare. It signals that the moment in front of you matters and that the outcome could carry weight. Courage doesn't require erasing fear; it requires putting fear on the table as part of your decision-making process. When fear shows up, don't retreat. Pause, name it, examine it, and let it inform—not dictate—your choice.

THE GOAL OF THIS CALL TO ACTION

To reframe fear as a *decision-making prerequisite* rather than an obstacle—one you actively engage with, analyze, and use as a catalyst for growth and meaningful action.

HOW TO BRING IT TO LIFE

1. **Locate and name your fear precisely:** Write down exactly what you're afraid of. Be specific. "I'm scared of failing" becomes "I'm afraid that if my idea flops, my colleagues will see me as less competent."
2. **Separate discomfort from danger:** Our fear system is wired to overreact. Ask: *is this truly dangerous or just uncomfortable?* This one question disrupts both bias (snap judgments) and exaggeration (unreal situations).
3. **Check the facts:** List factual evidence *for* and *against* the feared outcome. This forces logic to balance instinct.
4. **Run a best-/worst-case scan:** What's the worst that could realistically happen—and could you live with it? What's the best thing that could happen—and is it worth the risk?
5. **Visualize retreat:** If you walked away from this moment, what opportunity, growth, or impact would you be giving up?

6. **Step in, gradually:** Like firefighters, train before the blaze. For example, if public speaking terrifies you, start in front of a mirror, then a friend, then a small group—expanding your "comfort zone" in stages.

KEY ENABLERS OR CHALLENGES TO BE MINDFUL OF

- **Fear thrives in vagueness:** Naming it reduces its grip.
- **Bias distorts risk:** Your instincts aren't always right—fact-check them.
- **Discomfort ≠ danger:** Don't let your body's alarm bells override the bigger picture.
- **Small steps build capacity:** Incremental exposure makes fear manageable.
- **Courage compounds:** Each time you step toward fear, you make the next step easier.

Let fear walk beside you but never ahead of you. Each time you move toward it, you weaken its grip and strengthen your own. Accept fear into conversations, and fear may speak—but you make the decisions.

CHAPTER 5

REJECT DISTRACTING VOICES

"Never be limited by other people's limited imaginations. If you adopt their attitudes, then the possibility won't exist because you'll have already shut it out... You can hear other people's wisdom, but you've got to reevaluate the world for yourself."

—MAE C. JEMISON

My dad was not a great singer, but he loved to sing. One of his joys was teaching us the many rhymes and songs he had picked up over his lifetime. I don't remember all the songs he taught us, but one[47] stuck in my mind all these years:

Dare to be a Daniel,
Dare to stand alone!
Dare to have a purpose firm!
Dare to make it known.

Dad was prophetic. That refrain has helped me in countless moments of pressure.

Several years ago, during a major transformation initiative, I provoked the wrath of a few senior leaders who did not like how I was evaluating and reporting their business performance in monthly updates to the CEO and his executive team. I received calls or visits from all of them, and none were pleasant conversations. One gentleman sat across from me in my office and promised, "You have no idea with whom you are dealing. I can destroy you." I shrugged. Another let out that he could start a negative whisper campaign against me. I was aghast. Another bragged to me how rich and successful he already was and that silly reports from a "pipsqueak" did not matter to him. I was unimpressed. They wanted me to present a rosier picture of their work, but my duty was to give leadership accurate, unvarnished information, so I held firm.

I don't pretend to be anything like Daniel, but the hymn, which I now sing for my own children, does generate feelings and emotions that resonate with me. If you have dared to practice courage, it likely resonates with you too. You have not been thrown to the lions like Daniel was, but surely you have been ridiculed or called *crazy* for going against the grain, of not falling in line with others' dictates to you.

Choosing courage often means choosing to diverge from or oppose other views. It's not easy to do; sometimes it feels downright impossible—especially as opinionated as society sometimes is about what is considered *normal*. The voices in the crowd can get loud, aggressive, and intrusive. After I had left adidas and my family had returned to the US, I remember one person asking me which brand of car I drove. My Honda CRV did not go over very well. "Seriously? A big baller like you should be driving a BMW." (I was not a big baller.)

This might be the biggest challenge of all: to live courageously and make the choices that are in your best interest, not what others prefer. Even if you're armed with a strong purpose, even if you own your potential, even if you're ready to face your fears, you can still get derailed by listening to the wrong voices. Your mission can be detoured or derailed in an instant by one statement from a domineering, distracting voice that you allow to influence you. And the number one reason that people don't stay true to their purpose is because of the pressure, guidance, or expectations of others.

Allow me to be blunt: you cannot be courageous if you care about what everyone thinks about you, if you need to be popular, or if you have a craving to always be affirmed, coddled, or praised. It just doesn't work that way. If you choose to espouse courage, then be prepared to be misunderstood, called crazy, or worse. Your ability to be independent or filter out the voices and opinions of others is directly correlated with the impact you can have. Simply put, the more popular you feel you need to be, the less courageous you will be.

The Edelman Trust Barometer is an annual global survey that measures the level of trust that people have in various institutions, including businesses, governments, NGOs, and media across multiple countries. This survey has shown a consistent decline in trust in the US government, and the trend has accelerated in recent years.[48] If you wonder why this is the case, pay closer attention to our leaders. They represent a mangled cacophony of shifting principles, conflicted ideals, incessant double-talk, and an ill-conceived obsession with popularity. As a result, they do not represent a compelling picture of courage. It's hard to serve multiple masters—courage favors those who are willing to stand for something and buck the trend. If that is not your thing, then neither is courage! I know. You are immediately thinking about the tension between what you just read and history's fraternity of despots and their sycophants. Remember what I said in Chapter 1—true courage is virtuous.

It is never too early, or too late, to start acting from your conviction and dismiss the mob of voices around you—most of the time, they are mere distractions.

CALL ME CRAZY

Just a few months shy of finishing secondary school, I informed my parents that I would change my course of study when I entered university from natural sciences to social sciences, essentially abandoning my field of study for the previous four years. This was an unusual move given that I had been doing well in the track thought of as the best one for the so-called "smart students." But the reality was that over time I found myself more fascinated by courses like economics, business, and sociology than physics, chemistry, and additional mathematics. The cost of making this switch was going in a different direction from my tight group of friends and losing one year of placement in university. My parents and few others were understanding, but most others were incredulous. "How could you walk away from a respected field of study, only a few months shy of university and after spending so much time on it?" "Why would you want to take longer to graduate from university?" they asked. "You are *crazy*!"

I have gotten used to being called *unorthodox* in the years and decades since. When at the University of Sierra Leone, I used my free time outside of school to write application essays to US schools in pursuit of elusive scholarships. "Good luck," I was *teased*, and I was close to giving up until that night when I heard my mom's voice in the dark and my life changed forever.

I was called *foolish* for taking Dr. Guy's religion elective at Morehouse, because a C grade was the best anyone typically got out of it. I really wanted to learn about world religions and felt I could do the demanding work to earn better than a C, and I did. "There are easier courses," I was told. I earned a B. And my exposure to Buddhism in that class kindled a lasting interest in Asian cultures. For that, I would gladly have accepted a C.

The 1990s was a bonanza period for investment banking mega deals. While everyone in my Lehman Brothers analyst class was vying for the "hot" industry placements—technology, healthcare, telecommunications—I opted to throw my hat in for the unattractive Industrials Group, and *some laughed*. But I was more attracted to the consumer product clients covered in the group. Also, the team was much leaner than others, so I got to work on more assignments and get more deal exposure than analysts in the better-staffed teams.

When I requested a transfer from New York to work in Lehman's San Francisco office, I was called a *glutton for punishment* because the Bay Area team was known to be overworked. The stint was nowhere as bad as my classmates in New York had foretold, and I ended up working on fascinating technology, healthcare, and internet deals during the dot-com boom. And it turned out that Gap, Inc.—one of the hottest companies in the world then—was a few blocks away, and I was ultimately hired there.

And, oh, I did get to work for Goldman Sachs full-time after getting my MBA but left the role within a year of joining the company because it was a poor personal and cultural fit. When I walked into my team staffer's office to break the news, his reaction was not positive. Rather than letting his words distract me, I took it as confirmation for why I wanted to leave. "You are leaving the number one bank on The Street in the middle of a global recession?" he sneered. "*You've gone mad!*" Maybe I had. But that decision led to my career in the sports and lifestyle fashion industry.

Call me crazy for following my heart.

In all, I have worked for and left six organizations over the course of my career, each time after deep deliberation about what was important to me. Everyone did not always understand my decisions. At each transition, there was always a group that had lots of critical or negative things to say.

Notwithstanding the strong judgment and feedback, I enjoyed a career that exposed me to innovative work and amazing people. It also provided our family with enriching memories from around the globe. This diversity of work and life experience is an asset that is invaluable today when I advise companies as a consultant or board director.

And yes, when I decided five years ago to launch Custament Partners and focus on board governance, teaching, and consulting, *eyes rolled again*. "How could you give up so much potential when you are so close to the top?" people asked. By now, you know why—I was evolving into a fulfilling life by being my authentic and true self and daring to make vastly different choices than in the past.

I transitioned to each new role with no regrets, even if with some fear and trepidation, but was always at peace with my decisions. From the outside, it looked like I was making rash choices. I decided to do things that others would not have done, might not have considered, or simply did not understand. It did not seem to matter that my life was different from theirs. They still called me *crazy*, or maybe I am, just a little. I made some decisions because I was unwilling to trade my personal well-being for professional safety, tolerate a poor cultural fit, or be taken for granted at work. And since my family and the people who really mattered supported my choices, I took the leap despite the risks. Others had much to say and think, as they generally will, but they weren't the ones who really mattered. Their voices were only distractions I needed to reject to live out my purpose. Remember though, that these are courageous choices that I use here to make a point. I made lots of other fearful choices at other times. As I said, courage is a messy pilgrimage.

WE ARE ALL TRIBAL

Most people, especially those living in developed nations, do not normally view themselves as tribal. Most think of tribal people as something distant and exotic.

But we are all tribal by nature, even if we don't realize it. Our instincts lead us to join and identify with groups—family groups, friend groups, political groups, professional groups, religious groups, ethnic groups, interest groups, and more. These are tribes too. They provide a sense of belonging and create their own rituals and expectations. They have pressures, punishments, and codes of conduct—and those group norms have a decidedly strong influence on our behavior.

A 2014 study led by the University of Exeter found that a natural desire to be part of the "in crowd" could damage our ability to make the right decisions, and cited research that individuals have evolved to be overly influenced by their neighbors, rather than relying on their own instinct.[49]

That's not to say that belonging to a group is a dreadful thing. Groups are essential sources of support, knowledge, shared purpose, and identity. Our group memberships help anchor our identities as individuals. These social bonds are also crucial to our physical and mental health—chronic loneliness has been linked to depression, anxiety, and even early mortality. As I recently heard during talks by Colorado's Attorney General on the opioid crisis in America, "The opposite of addiction is not sobriety. It is community." It may not be a quote original to him, but I have heard him use it multiple times.[50] As humans, we need to feel a sense of belonging.

That said, the problems often start when the group's values, goals, and rules don't align with our personal sense of purpose. That pits our desire for belonging and social cohesion against our desire for personal fulfillment. What should be a both/and becomes an either/or, and our evolutionary nature as social animals makes it easy to let group influence overshadow personal agency.

Sometimes, going along with the group is a relatively benign choice. Only a few weeks after I started college in Atlanta, the weather turned slightly chilly. At a local mall where I worked, I noticed that almost all the young people my age were wearing an identical garment—a coarse, woven, blanket-like poncho. I remember musing to myself: Had I missed the memo about the uniform of the day? Why would so many different people all wear the same wardrobe item on the same day?

At other times, going along with the group is more consequential and needs to be more intentional. When we look back at human civilization, it becomes obvious that progress often begins with one person or small group making a sharp break from what's accepted. This is what brought about the end of slavery, independence from colonialism, women's access to voting, and many other movements from which we have all benefited. These movements and their leaders were met with fierce resistance from the majority. Leaders and their followers were threatened, attacked, imprisoned, and murdered—all the most extreme forms of social rejection. And yet they persisted in pursuing their purpose.

What made this possible? Courage.

In our lives, the choice between following the crowd and going our own way will probably not be so dramatic. That doesn't make it any easier—in fact, it might make it harder. Rebelling against a clear villain is a straightforward choice. It's not only the obvious thing to do, but it's also the right thing to do. Rejecting the well-meaning advice of people who are close to us—people we trust and care about—feels much more complicated and certainly takes just as much, if not more, courage.

Social influence can subtly (or not so subtly) steer every aspect of our lives, how we dress, how we talk, where we live, who we socialize with, how we spend our time and money, and much more. Some of that influence is helpful, even positive...but sometimes it undermines our ability to become the person we want to be. To know the difference, we first need to examine the sources and motivations of influence in our lives.

TRIBES BY BIRTH AND TRIBES BY CHOICE

We are born into some groups. These are fixed categories based on our ethnicity, place of birth, or family. I am from Sierra Leone, for example, and will always be from Sierra Leone. I was raised by middle-class, Protestant parents, of an ethnic group descended from enslaved Africans who were liberated and settled in Freetown during the abolition movement.[51] I did not choose Sierra Leone as my nation or the middle class as my socioeconomic group or formerly enslaved as my family narrative. I inherited these memberships by being born into the Williams family.

We join other groups through our own choices over our lifetimes. These include our career path, our interests, where we live, and so on. Think about it: Who are your colleagues, friends, and neighbors? Who do you identify with through shared beliefs or interests, even if you don't interact with them personally, like alumni groups (e.g., Oregon Ducks or Oregon State Beavers), political groups (e.g., Republicans or Democrats) or lifestyle movements (e.g., vegetarians or dragon boat racers)? Mine include Morehouse Men, Harvard graduates, employee groups of some of the companies I worked for, Black cycling groups, Americans in the Netherlands, and many, many more.

Further, consider the groups you have belonged to over the course of your life, and you'll see that your choice of groups has changed at least a little bit. As you grow, you get exposed to diverse ways of thinking and living. As you gain knowledge and experience, you may find yourself gravitating toward new tribes, and this may mean that you distance yourself from old ones or leave them behind altogether. This happens naturally as you move through various stages of life, and sometimes, you'll find you need to stand up to them.

STANDING UP TO OUR TRIBES

All said, it is one thing to be part of a tribe and a completely different thing for it to drive, or make, all your decisions for you. True, taking a stand against the expectations and norms of a group takes a lot of courage because the consequences can be harsh—censure, retribution, even banishment from the group. History is littered with examples of courageous people who stood up to their tribes and paid the price. Martin Luther was excommunicated from the Catholic Church for inspiring the Protestant Reformation and forced into hiding until his death twenty-five years later.[52] For challenging the scientific beliefs of his day, Galileo was sentenced to house arrest, where he remained for the rest of his life, nine years, until his death in 1642.[53] In the wake of the September 11 attacks on the United States, then congressperson Barbara Lee was the only member of Congress to vote against the authorization of use of force, a move that was deeply unpopular and subjected her to scorn for years after.[54]

But even on a less dramatic scale, the consequences of standing up to your tribe can hurt. We all know of people who have been estranged from their families over coming out of the closet with their sexual orientation or revealing their gender identity. Or we have heard about those who have lost friends over political disagreements. Even positive achievements like academic or financial success can cause rifts if the people around you begin to resent you for your success or do not fully understand your choices and decisions. Losing these social ties causes real pain, even if they don't land you in jail or ostracize you.

We also have institutionalized tribalism around the world. Try getting a mortgage when you don't work for an established company or have a nontraditional income stream. Or walk into some buildings without the right hairstyle or style of dress. It's not easy. As a global society we have designed structures and standards that are not friendly to outliers. It is hard to be different. It takes conscious and determined effort. It takes courage. It's even harder when your difference is inimical (we'll talk about this in Chapter 8).

Even when we're not actively standing against something, society can reprimand us in unexpected ways for departing from the norm. When I decided to leave traditional corporate work and become an independent consultant, professional clubs that had courted me suddenly lost interest because my impressive corporate title was no longer current. They no longer saw me as part of their tribe.

That said, separating yourself from the pack is often a good thing, especially for the reasons that this book is about.

Making the point another way, it is a comparable situation in the business world, where the most successful companies are those that stand out, not those that imitate others. The latter can succeed for a time, but they typically end up struggling to keep up with a changing or competitive world. The ones that become household names are the ones that dare to be different and become both more relevant and more respected for their uniqueness.

Earlier, I introduced the Edelman Trust Barometer. In addition to showing us that people are losing trust in governments around the globe, it reveals that business leaders are generally trusted more than other institutional leaders.[55] In the 2024 report, business was viewed with a significant lead over government in both competence and ethics, but notably even this trust is eroding slowly and is expected to be tested even more, as the public perceives businesses are becoming more misaligned with its own values. For example, in the wake of George Floyd's killing, global corporations oscillated between supporting environmental, social, and governance initiatives to rejecting them and sweeping them under the rug in response to political pressures and cultural crosswinds only a few years after. Often, our courage or lack of it is on full display for others to see, so whether we—institutions or individuals—actively build a reputation for courage or shrink from big decisions opportunistically does matter over time.

One thing I found in my research for this book is that history tends to sort out courage from cowardice and capitulation from conviction. It takes more effort to differentiate yourself, but it gets easier with practice, and once you become known as an independent spirit, you often find less resistance from others. Others might even begin to imitate *you* or seek you out for your objective counsel.

In the previous chapter, we discussed how fear can get in our way if we don't put it in check. The same is true of distracting voices if we don't learn to stand up to them. The courage to do what we believe is right doesn't magically blossom in the moment of challenge. If we haven't already been practicing courage in small ways, we'll find it difficult to rise to the challenge, especially when the stakes are high.

Here are a couple of ways to train yourself to be independent and vigilant, so you could stand up to a tribe, if the need arises.

LEARN TO HAVE DIFFICULT CONVERSATIONS

One important way to practice is to develop the skill of having difficult conversations.[56] By learning to manage conflict and confrontation without destroying relationships, we'll become more comfortable with saying "no" to things that we find unacceptable.

This was the situation in which a coalition of interfaith leaders found themselves, in March 1965. On March 7, 1965, people around the world saw televised images of Bloody Sunday—the brutal beatings of six hundred unarmed civil rights protestors attempting to peacefully march across the Edmund Pettus Bridge in Alabama. Quickly, a second march was organized, with Dr. Martin Luther King, Jr., himself leading the way. A call went out across the nation for citizens and clergy to join them in the march. Secular and holy men and women of all faiths and races from across the country who had slowly been growing apart from their tribes on the issue of racial segregation decided to show up at that moment. The need for their presence and moral support had become impossible to ignore. The role of this interfaith coalition is not often talked about. Especially in light of another overlooked fact. At the time he was alive, Dr. Martin Luther King, Jr., was not as popular and well-received as today's acclaim of him makes it out. I read somewhere that he polled in the twenties. So those religious leaders were not exactly aligned with their flock. And their courage made a difference.[57]

One of the hardest things about standing up to others is choosing the moment to do it, especially if we've been going along with the crowd for a while. Often, the sense of discomfort grows slowly, and some kind of trigger is needed to nudge us into action—a moment of choice that forces us to pick an opposing position from the tribe and have a hard talk with its members about it.

BEING HYPERSENSITIVE TO TRIBES GOING EXTREME

Sometimes, tribes do go rogue. As you know by now, I lived in Germany for a few years. I enjoyed its people and the culture, and it was always difficult to comprehend that the beautiful country and its people that played host to us were, only two generations ago, in a face-off with the rest of Europe and much of the world in an ugly war that illustrated the worst of tribalism.

Germany's gift to all of us is the lasting reminder that standing up to our tribe is something which life events could call upon us to do. How could one man lead so many people astray?

Dietrich Bonhoeffer, a German theologian and anti-Nazi dissident, offers some of the most searing critiques of collective passivity. He addressed the concept of "stupidity" (his word, not mine), in his posthumously published *Letters and Papers from Prison*.[58] He defined it as the tendency of ordinary people, under the sway of power, social or political pressure to lose their independence and ability to exercise critical thinking, leaving them susceptible to manipulation. Bonhoeffer saw the phenomenon as not merely a lack of intelligence but as a deeper moral failing—an inability or unwillingness to critically engage with truth or take responsibility for one's actions. Strong language aside, Bonhoeffer echoes some important themes in this book—namely, the power of the individual with moral clarity and courage to know when to challenge the tribe and how the consequences could be dire when this power is not exercised.

To conclude the point—groups can turn bad, and we need tons of courage to make ourselves aware when this is happening and to dissociate from them.

How then do you decide when to disengage from a tribe?

PULLING AWAY FROM A TRIBE

It's not always simple. But to know when to tune out your tribe, you may want to look for red flags—group behaviors that are likely to create friction with your own instincts. Here are some of these red flags:

- **Goodthink or "For the good of the group"**: When groups justify harmful behavior by saying it's necessary to help or protect the group, be careful. You could find yourself tempted to act against your values to preserve your standing.
- **Deindividuation or "That's how we do things here"**: When members fully buy into the expectations of the tribe and lose their sense of identity and personal responsibility, they're more likely to participate in negative behaviors that become acceptable to the group—like rioting with hundreds of other sports fans after their team loses.

- **Groupshift or "We thought you were committed":** This occurs when a slight tendency among members becomes exaggerated in a group setting. If members are slightly risk-tolerant, they might engage in highly risky behaviors together. Even minor biases can be amplified in this way.
- **Groupthink or "Leadership has decided—align":** This happens when members begin to agree on every issue out of a desire for harmony. Nobody wants to be a rabble-rouser, so they acquiesce publicly even if they complain privately. It's common in the corporate world, where collaboration can slide into conformity at the expense of effectiveness. Beware.

It won't be easy to leave or confront the tribe. In fact, it can be quite risky. But that is what courage is all about. So, when you start to feel uncomfortable with the direction your tribe is heading, keep an eye out for those moments of decision—even if they mean "quitting."

SOMETIMES, QUITTING IS FOR WINNERS

A quick word on quitting. It is quite common for people to believe that they are *not quitters*, embrace this with pride, and subsequently stay in bad situations longer than they need to. Quitting is not always the wrong decision. Moving from a familiar but tricky situation to an unfamiliar one with greater potential isn't quitting or giving up—even if you've invested heavily in the first path. It takes courage, and you will be challenged to make choices like this many times in your life. How you handle these calls could make *a difference* for you. Any of these calls could make *the difference* that you need. Hunkering down in the bad status quo is not laudable and nothing to be proud of. It is often the opposite of courage.

When is it the right time to quit? If you can't gain traction in an environment despite your best efforts and have trouble building a support system that will help you thrive, it might be a sign that you're in the wrong environment. It may not even be a negative environment—just not a *positive* one that supports what you vision for your future. If you are in an organization where no one shares or understands your purpose, it will be harder to find people you can count on and trust. If you are part of a group whose habitual inclinations run afoul of your values and there is nothing you can do to influence its tendencies, then yes, you must seriously reconsider your membership in that group.

When I worked at Gap, a senior executive once advised me to only stay in situations where I felt respected and valued because only then would I do my best work, be rewarded for it, and feel energized to give more. She was onto something that I didn't fully understand at the time, but I certainly do now. Most times, we are quitting a dire situation, which is different from quitting on ourselves.

Every time I've changed jobs in my career journey, it was because I needed a change of atmosphere. I don't think of those decisions as "quitting" in the sense of having a low resilience threshold. They were calculated choices to break away from a tribe that no longer fit or conditions and values that were not conducive or helpful to my goals, which is something to be celebrated. If you feel alone, even in a crowd, and find it increasingly hard to be your authentic self, it's probably time for a change of scenery.

I mentioned before that I resigned from my role at Goldman Sachs because it was a poor cultural fit. Although it was "at the worst possible time," my world did not collapse, contrary to the dire predictions of my staffer, some colleagues, and others. A few months later, I rejoined the corporate headquarters at Gap. I took a 70 percent pay cut, but I was 1,000 percent happier with the work I was doing and the people I was doing it with. Being back in a more diverse environment, among creatives, and in a corporate community that was humbler and that actively engaged with real consumers and supported social issues was more my tribe. Over the years, building on the move, I ended up getting hired by several similarly established companies in the lifestyle fashion, sports, and retail industries and would spend the rest of my corporate career in the sector, up until my departure from adidas Group in December 2018.

I look back and feel gratitude that I was strong enough in these moments to ignore the mob and take the forks in the road that I did, despite the second-guessers. I would have been miserable had I remained a banker, and my life would have evolved in ways that I would rather not think about today. In the end, I enjoyed an illustrious career, and those voices that made it seem like I was crazy just melted away, no doubt to find other victims to influence.

Don't let situations where it's clear that you need to stand up to naysayers or quit pass you by—these are your opportunities to practice courage in a big way. And you will likely need it because it may even be necessary to leave the comfort of long-affiliated tribes. It's a scary transition, to be sure, but it's not the end of the world. In fact, it could be necessary for your sanity and growth.

COURAGE PILGRIM IN ACTION
JANET KING (SINGLE MOM OF FIVE BOYS)

"Let me be."

It seems like for much of her eight decades on earth, Janet Luciana King faced detractors, battled with them, and invariably proved them wrong. She was born in 1894, in colonial era Nigeria, to a Sierra Leonean father on a British government assignment. From the outset, as an outsider in her birth country, little Janet decided that even if "no" would be a word she would hear a lot, it wouldn't be one that defined her. When her father returned home, he left her behind in Nigeria under the care of her maternal relatives, but not for long. He worried about her educational prospects given that, traditionally, the attitude toward girls' education was "no." No, he decided, his daughter would get an education, so he moved her to join him in Sierra Leone. However, his wife was not keen on her husband's out-of-wedlock daughter living with them and said "no," and Janet ended up in a foster home, where she remained for much of her early life.

While her father supported her financially, Janet learned to be independent in her new home, developing leadership skills not only in the household but also in the community at large. She completed primary school, but when her secondary education faltered, she took to petty trading in local markets to earn money. She had a knack for business, was disciplined, worked hard, and soon gained respect for her savvy. As her stature grew, so did her sense of self-worth and her independence. Her purpose, she determined early in life, was to build the best life she could for herself and defy all the odds to the contrary. And the life she envisioned would be a good one for her children as well. Nothing and no one was going to stop her.

She married at an early age to a customs officer who was often assigned roles in faraway provincial areas, so Janet was forced to parent two young boys on her own. Upon her marriage, her father transferred to her the savings he had set aside, and the young bride found herself under pressure from her husband to turn the funds over to him, which was not unusual for the time. No. She refused, and he, in turn, stopped providing financial assistance to run the home. Undeterred, Janet used the money to buy a house in her name and rented it out for income.

By this time, Janet had learned the need for self-reliance in a patriarchy. She reasoned that living modestly and within her means empowered her, and she understood the importance of building a healthy and supportive community around her and her children. She became known for her generosity, wisdom, and perspective. And her independence. All this, despite her many difficult challenges.

Things took a turn when her husband fell ill with typhoid, died on assignment, and was buried in a grave she was never able to locate. She missed his funeral because she was pregnant with her third child. At twenty-seven, with limited formal education and three boys to raise, she applied for death benefits from the government and was offered a paltry sum, net of taxes. She responded in a way that was unheard of at that time. No. She wrote an appeal to the colonial Governor (effectively the head of state) with an emphatic disagreement, making a case for a tax exemption due to hardship, which was approved—the first time this had ever happened. Janet never remarried, though she had two more boys, whom she raised alone. She dealt with the stigma of being a single mom of five boys, rejecting good-intentioned advice to find a new husband, even as she continually struggled with those who questioned her standing and ability to advocate for her sons. "No," she said, even when bank loans without a male guarantor were not an option.

Janet's courage and independence paid off. She was strong and respected. Family and neighbors alike would send their kids over to help with chores and, eventually, to live with her and learn from her. Her house became a foster home of sorts. For decades until her old age, grandchildren, children of relatives, and children of neighbors became part- or full-time members of her household and regarded her as Mom. Long after she passed away in 1980, she is still remembered for her strong personality. Her "no" wasn't rebellion for its own sake; it was alignment to purpose under pressure.

Janet's five boys grew to become successful professionals, as did many of her wards, foster children, and grandchildren, including my own mother, my mom's siblings, and their cousins. Janet was my maternal great-grandmother.

BUILDING A STRONG INNER CIRCLE

Despite these moments when you need to go your own way, I hope you do not take away the message that you need to take on life alone. This couldn't be further from the truth. Everyone needs someone who supports them on their journey to their courageous self. We are not islands unto ourselves. We are neither all-knowing nor do we have all the resources and access we need to succeed. We have many gaps and blind spots. So we need support, advice, and direction from others to help us see more clearly. But we must see them as working for us and not the other way around. These are the voices we not only want but need to hear.

The best protection against unhelpful and distracting social influence is our own appointed support system. We must seek out and connect with people who have a beneficial effect on us and who we know will back us in pursuing our purpose. These are trusted people whom we can turn to for guidance and emotional support at any time and be assured of direct but uplifting feedback. I call this my inner circle.

So who's in your inner circle? You can consider them your personal advisory board. These could be people with whom you have a long or strong relationship. Or they could be members of your network that you seek out or rely on from time to time. Your family could be part of your inner circle too. The only requirement of them all is that you trust them to give honest advice that places your interests front and center.

For example, my innermost circle includes my wife, mother, brothers and sister, several childhood friends, a former boss from Nike, a former colleague from adidas, a former administrator from my undergraduate alma mater, and a professional coach who is more of a friend.

My siblings know me better than anyone; we had the same upbringing, even if we have different career paths. Henderson, my younger brother, is a professional chef, a great listener, completely nonjudgmental, full of pragmatic insights, and completely family devoted. He is not a corporate clone, which makes his perspective valuable when I need just common-sense advice. My mom is ever available and, like Henderson, always a reliable source of refreshing insights that come from outside my professional world.

Six of my closest childhood peers and I exchange texts daily. They are the same guys I "parted company" with thirty-five years ago in high school when I decided to become a social scientist. We also meet for a weekend every year and counsel each other nonstop. We understand each other's Sierra Leonean roots and subsequent journeys and have been friends since the 1970s and '80s.

Gary, my former boss—one of my closest advisors and most ardent supporters—has a measured, thoughtful, and objective way of thinking that I've always respected and benefited from. He gives feedback that is both honest and constructive without ever being pessimistic or unrealistic. The same can be said of Michael, with whom I worked at adidas and came to trust the moment I first met him.

In our professional and personal lives, many of us have benefited from mentors, sponsors, career coaches, and therapists, and while they all factor into our success model, I speak of my inner circle with some distinction. I've chosen these people intentionally, not by default or chance. These are the voices I most need to hear. I trust them because they know me well and fully support my purpose. And they would all go to bat for me—ours is not a transactional relationship.

When I was named the President of African Leadership University, John, a former executive at Morehouse College who then worked at Harvard University, had me visit him in Boston. Over the course of a long day, we visited several university leaders in the Boston area, whom John had asked to curate words of advice for me.

The experience was a huge boost to my knowledge and confidence on the eve of the important role, thanks to John and his network. An inner circle will do that—go to bat for you even if you don't ask.

Once someone becomes a part of your inner circle, they will hopefully be a part of your journey for years to come...but not necessarily forever. Your paths may diverge at some point, and that's okay. Allow yourself to be flexible and change your team over time.

The voices that help you on your courage journey do not all have to be from a fixed or closed membership either. As needed on your courage journey, you can also reach out to experts outside of the circle if you require specialized advice on a specific topic. When I decided to take African Leadership University into lockdown in March 2020, I remember one of my trusted confidants, Jim, walking over to me and saying, "You did the right thing." It was reassuring—Jim was not only trusted but eminently qualified—a veteran of public relations and crises, including serving as a senior advisor and spokesperson for US Airways following the 2009 crash of Flight 1549 into the Hudson River (The Miracle on the Hudson).[59]

So yes, the core group would be quite small, but continuously adding or relying on other people, as needed, who can have your ear and help you with specific subjects is the best way to courageous decision-making. And if push comes to shove, the whisper in your ear could come even from complete strangers who are well-placed to give you advice or counsel. The key points to remember are that you are not an island, but at the same time you have the final call and must get good at deciding who has your ear.

BENEFITS OF A STRONG INNER CIRCLE

If you build a strong group of advisors who understand and support you, you'll enjoy some clear benefits. You'll have better information, more encouragement, and a stronger feeling of security. You'll find it easier to act courageously because you'll be strengthened and reassured by their voices...if you listen to them.

PROCESSING RISK

I once advised a startup, and against the better judgment of my inner circle, I got maybe too emotionally involved with the venture and, soon thereafter, financially involved. My inner circle kept warning me to keep my exuberance for the company at arm's length, but I kept foolishly treating *their* voices as distractions. It turned out my inner circle was right. The startup's founders had mismanaged the business and lacked the maturity to lead it forward, eventually alienating their investors and dooming the venture. It was a letdown, especially as I had been one of their strongest advocates, publicly praising and defending them. The point I am making is even if you first ignore glaring danger signs in the form of your own inner voice, listen to the inner circle around you, especially if you have chosen them wisely and you trust them unreservedly. Learning to filter the voices takes practice and trial and error. Ultimately, it's up to you to decide who you listen to, and this will not always go as hoped.

SPOTTING OPPORTUNITY

One of the greatest benefits of a strong inner circle is that it allows you to discover yourself through their eyes. As we grow and come into our own, we never get a letter in the mail that says, "Dear Christopher, you were once a lowly specialist when you graduated from college, but you have now developed the abilities of a strong emerging executive. This is the time for you to be more confident and claim bigger goals or ask for more responsibilities." No one gets a notice like that, but your inner circle is the next best thing to help you become self-aware. It's sometimes hard to see yourself accurately, especially as you change slowly over time and are consumed each day with getting work and life done. Your inner circle is removed from your daily minutiae and can act as a mirror that shows how you are growing and what you're truly capable of, and encourages you to stretch your limits even more. They can help you find courage just as much as others might act to extinguish it. That's a great inner circle at work—one that upsizes you when you have not realized that you are overdue for it!

Realize that to enjoy these benefits you must do the work to get the most out of your inner circle:

- **Be willing to open up and share.** That is the only way they can help you connect dots that you might not be seeing.
- **Be vulnerable.** Ask for help and admit what you know and don't know. False bravado can only take you so far. No one wants to help a know-it-all.
- **Have an open mind.** Be ready to hear them out and adopt an open mind for out-of-the-box thinking. Remember, courage is all about stepping out of your comfort zone.
- **Keep them updated.** Ensure that your inner circle is kept abreast of the updates in your life so that they are always operating on the best information about you.
- **Express your gratitude often.** Show gratitude for their efforts by sending short update notes or recognizing events in their lives. Show them that you care and appreciate the relationship, and that you're not a leech or thinking only transactionally.

FILTERING THE NOISE

All day, every day, you are bombarded with messages about what you should and shouldn't do. Some are as obvious as praise from your boss or pressure from a relative. Others are more subtle—everything from the ads you see while scrolling on social media to the way the people around you dress and talk contains some kind of message about what is considered good and what is not.

You might not be able to avoid *hearing* these messages, but it's your choice whether to *listen*. When people offer their opinions, guidance, advice, and observations, don't just take them—filter them. You get to decide whether they're important to you and whether to let them affect your decisions.

This is especially true when you get negative feedback—when someone criticizes, rejects, or questions your ideas and actions. Now, some criticism is perfectly valid and even helpful. But over the years, I've noticed a few types of criticism that should be taken with a big grain of salt or even ignored completely:

- **Hostile:** This criticism is purely negative, often demeaning, and intended to stop you in your tracks. It usually comes from people who feel threatened, see life as a zero-sum game, and resent the success of others. I once shared a writing draft with a respected author who responded this way, and I never trusted them again.
- **Conservative:** This feedback is overcautious and rooted in a scarcity mindset. These critics avoid risk, cling to what they have, and try to pull you into their comfort zone, often steering you away from your own goals. It's easy to follow this group because risk aversion is so alluring.
- **Traditional:** These critics resist change, not out of fear but from a preference for the status quo. They rarely see a need for deviation or new scenarios and almost never take the lead in making things happen. These people are normally institutionalist and need directions from the top. Nietzsche cautioned about this in Chapter 1.
- **Limited:** This criticism comes from a lack of imagination. The

person focuses on constraints and unrealistic hypotheticals, and often only supports change after it is already underway. They are often well-meaning but best suited as supporters from the back row, not as advisors who have your ear.
- **Undermining:** These are gatekeepers who never acknowledge your readiness for a bigger opportunity, shifting the goalposts to keep you feeling insufficient. They never see you as ready or able, no matter what you do. This is the boss who never wants to talk about a promotion, not exactly hostile but always an unhelpful naysayer.
- **Trolls:** These are the peanut gallery—uninformed, loud, and often anonymous. They rely on clichés and mob logic, and they tear others down for sport. The best response is to ignore them completely.

FINAL WORDS—CHOOSE YOUR INFLUENCERS INTENTIONALLY

As social beings, the desire to belong is natural. Yet the wrong choice is to allow the external chatter—the opinions, fears, or expectations of others—a disproportionate place in your process or to outsource to it your sense of direction. That path blurs your purpose and dilutes your potential.

The courageous choice is to remain anchored in your own voice. Your experiences, the lessons you have drawn from them, and your vision of a fulfilling life are uniquely yours. No one else carries the same perspective or responsibility for your purpose. When you let the voices of others become louder than your own, you surrender the steering wheel of your life. But when you discern wisely—welcoming voices that offer encouragement and helpful perspectives, and rejecting those that cloud or diminish—you preserve clarity and strengthen conviction.

Rejecting distracting voices is not about walking alone; it is about choosing your company intentionally. It is building a circle of people who sharpen you without overshadowing you, who challenge you without silencing you, and who remind you of your own power when doubt creeps in. As astronaut Mae C. Jemison advised, you can learn from the wisdom of others while still reevaluating the world for yourself.

Courage means filtering the noise so that your true voice leads the way. With that clarity in place, you are ready for the next step: to translate conviction into momentum. The next chapter, Chapter 6, turns to this essential practice—learning how to act decisively.

A CALL TO ACTION: SET A HIGH BAR FOR WHO INFLUENCES YOU

On the courage journey, every voice you let in will either sharpen your purpose or dull it. The point isn't to block out the world but to curate whose perspectives you allow to shape your decisions.

THE GOAL OF THIS CALL TO ACTION

To deliberately raise your standards for whose advice, feedback, and opinions you accept—ensuring that only the most trusted, purposeful voices have lasting influence on your choices.

HOW TO BRING IT TO LIFE

1. **Name your inner circle:** Identify the few people who truly know you, your purpose, and your values—and whose track record shows they want your success.
2. **Filter every voice:** Before taking advice, ask: Does this person understand my context? Do they have relevant experience? Have they shown courage in their own life?
3. **Spot hidden agendas:** Pay attention to whether someone's feedback serves your growth or protects their own comfort, ego, or control.
4. **Weigh their stake in your success:** Would they be invested in your achievement—or indifferent if you failed?
5. **Act with discernment:** Take in perspectives without giving everyone equal weight. Advice that doesn't align with your purpose gets tuned out or challenged.
6. **Be willing to cut ties:** If someone consistently undermines your values or direction, you have both the right and the responsibility to remove their influence.

KEY ENABLERS OR CHALLENGES TO BE MINDFUL OF

- **Not all well-intentioned feedback is good advice:** Evaluate it against your purpose, not the person's title or relationship to you.
- **The loudest voices aren't always the wisest:** Listen for the quiet speakers who are qualified over the loud voices that are not.
- **Curating influence isn't isolation:** It's selective listening in service of your purpose.
- **Be aware of the voices you allow close:** Your courage will grow in proportion to their clarity and helpfulness.

Guard the gates of your mind as carefully as you would a priceless treasure. The people you allow in will either elevate your courage or erode it—choose those whose presence calls you upward.

CHAPTER 6

ACT DECISIVELY

> "The credit belongs to the man who is actually in the arena...who errs, who comes short again and again...but who does actually strive to do the deeds."
>
> —THEODORE ROOSEVELT

It happened in an instant. One moment I was chatting with a senior executive at Nike about career opportunities and the next I had agreed to move to Southeast Asia and embark on one of the most transformative periods in my career.

I had been working for Nike in Portland, Oregon, for five years and had been in my current position overseeing Global Geographies strategy for almost four years. My job was fine, and I was enjoying the work. During my tenure, I helped conceive and oversee the implementation of the most significant corporate transformation the company had undertaken.

We shifted from region- and product-led business units to a three-dimensional matrix organization—six sport categories—layered on top of the legacy P&Ls. We called it Category Offense.[60]

In parallel, we reoriented wholesale and owned retail to reflect the category model at point of sale—we called this Marketplace Transformation. As the head of Global Geographies strategy, I helped lead this initiative and ensure its rollout across the regions.[61]

With Marketplace Transformation developed, approved by Nike's Board of Directors, and the three largest regions—North America, Western Europe, and Greater China—up and running, I was starting to feel stagnant and ready for a new challenge. I had long desired to become a General Manager with P&L responsibilities, leading one of our territories. Thankfully, the corporate culture at Nike also encouraged job changes every three years, so I was overdue for a move.

I met with one of the senior executives at the company, also a mentor to me, to discuss my potential options. He was, as always, supportive and spent an hour brainstorming with me about new opportunities. But before we wrapped up our meeting, another executive leaned into the office to have a quick word with him.

The visitor noticed me sitting on the sofa and asked, "What's Williams doing here?"

"I'm helping him figure out his next role," my mentor replied.

The other executive thought for a moment. "I might have something for you," he said. He was the head of Emerging Markets region for the company.

I leaned forward.

"My country manager in Malaysia just quit," he said. "That's a role you can consider. But beyond that, there is a lot going on in Southeast Asia. It's in line for a transformation, has high growth potential, and it's underperforming as well. The region needs someone to shake it up and help turn it around. They could use your help."

At the time, I was prioritizing one of the top three regions. Southeast Asia wasn't on my radar. I also had not had a conversation with my wife about any specific preferences she had. So I demurred. "That's interesting," I said. "I'll definitely think about it."

My mentor was incredulous. "You just sat in my office for an hour talking about needing a new opportunity. Then someone comes in and offers you a job that is completely new and different, with an opportunity to own your own P&L, and your response is, 'Let me think about it?'" He shook his head, frustrated.

I swallowed and smiled sheepishly and turned to the other executive and said, "Could you ask me again?"

"Do you want to move to Southeast Asia?"

"*Yes, I do*," I responded with emphasis.

I passed by him as I was walking out the door. He said, "Williams, if you really want this job, you need to be there by this weekend. The regional sales meeting is on Monday, and you will need to lead it."

I was a quick learner. "I'll be there," I said.

On the way back to my office, I called my wife. "I've been offered a job in Southeast Asia and the opportunity to also run Nike Malaysia," I told her.

"Did you take it?" She sounded excited.

"Yes!" Knowing immediately that I had her support, I was beginning to feel the excitement myself. "I have to head out this weekend."

She didn't miss a beat. "That's amazing!"

Less than a week later, I was in Southeast Asia and starting my new role.

Four months later, my wife left her role as an attending optometrist at a Portland, Oregon, hospital and joined me—landing in Singapore just after midnight on January 1, 2010.

Remember how, in the previous chapter, we talked about the importance of that inner circle and how it can help you push forward because it knows you so well? My wife has undoubtedly been one such person for as long as we have known each other. Notwithstanding her support, I tell this story to make another point: even with my strong, clear desire to take on a new role, I came close to missing an opportunity that turned out to be tailor-made for me. I'll unpack this decision a little later.

For now, I want the message to be clear—your courage comes to life only when you act!

TAKING ACTION

We've talked about many choices that promote courage in this book so far, but without question, after purpose, acting is the most essential choice in practicing *and* showing courage. We can only talk about courage for so long. At some point, it's time to act and show what you truly stand for.

Nothing expresses your true priorities and intentions like acting, and nothing but action can turn potential into reality. But it's also the hardest to master because it's where the rubber hits the road—where all your convictions (as we discussed in Chapter 2 about purpose and in Chapter 3 about confidence) are tested and where the demons of fear (that we discussed in Chapter 4) tend to reside. It is the progress that the discouraging mob (we discussed in Chapter 5) tries to steer you away from. For all these reasons, defaulting to action is a crucial skill in a courageous life. It is the single step that moves us from strategy to execution and from hope to accomplishment. It's the only way to turn everything you've learned so far into the fulfilling, authentic, impactful life you want. It is also the hill where many aspirations and good intentions die. And indeed, the way to avoid paralysis and stagnation is progress. As Lao Tzu, the Chinese philosopher said, "The journey of a thousand miles begins with one step."

Earlier in this book we discussed courage as having virtuous intent. An additional word here—virtue does not mean taking the high horse of judgment over others and then standing still. Professed morality and good intentions aside, courage does not miraculously appear in to-do lists, fervent promises, impassioned speeches, and thoughts and prayers. Rather, it emerges through actions founded upon these things. Courage is deliberate, alert to timing, and impact-oriented—it doesn't arrive late to the party with excuses. Actions matter—it is as plain and simple as that.

Everything we've talked about in this book has prepared you for this choice, for it is a choice—understanding why you must take the first step, and the next, and many more. It's time to learn the power of action and how to cultivate it as an enduring habit. But before we get there, it's important to see how we might try to get out of action and why our fears morph into a myriad of reasons and excuses to avoid it.

EIGHT COMMON EXCUSE PATTERNS

There's a fine line between reasons and excuses. Reasons lead to action; excuses defend inaction.

Here are a few excuse patterns, or saboteurs of action, that we have all likely employed.

"I'M NOT READY ENOUGH YET."

This excuse is clearly rooted in the fear of failure, which we will discuss at length in the next chapter. If this thought prevents you from acting, ask yourself: What would happen if that were true, and you did the thing anyway? What would the best- and worst-case performance scenarios for you look like? Chances are the worst case is not as dire as you imagine it to be.

You've likely heard motivational speakers admit, "I had no business receiving that task that I was assigned at a very young age, but I figured it out." They are right. You might not feel you are good enough for something, but when the moment picks you, I can promise that you are more ready than you think. Seize it.

You don't always have to be perfect for an opportunity. Sometimes all you need is to be *good enough* or *ready enough*!

"I NEED MORE INFORMATION."

Of course, information is crucial for making good decisions. However, it's easy to get bogged down in analysis and end up with paralysis. More information does not always lead to more clarity or more courage; it can also overwhelm and distract you from the crucial decision at hand. If you find yourself doing research to put off acting, it helps to focus on the essential factors of your choice.

What is the decision to be made or the action to be taken, and what single fact does it most rely on? Which information must you know for sure? What information can you do without? How much information is enough? What do your instincts tell you? When is action needed? You only need to do enough research to be informed about the most critical things—the rest is overthinking. Too many filters make weak coffee. Too much overthinking weakens courage.

Also, there is often a window of time when an action is most impactful. Be clear what that window is and act within it—stopping all research to decide and pursue your choice. We'll talk more about timing later.

"I HAVE OTHER PRIORITIES RIGHT NOW."

This may be genuinely true. But it's easy to use urgent priorities to put off important actions that are less time-sensitive and more difficult. I did this more than once during the writing of this book. I started brainstorming in 2019, writing in 2021, and published in 2025. Yes, several disruptive life events happened that demanded my immediate attention—the pandemic, the decline and passing of my dad, our family's relocation from Mauritius to the United

States and then to Europe. But there were many other distractions that could have been set aside or managed away so that I could get my book done. This is what it comes down to, though—writing can be tough, so I used those events and others as "reasons" to pause the book project—only to find that it was even harder to pick up the work again six months later. And here we are, six years later...

I recommend here the same trick I mentioned in the Introduction. Any time you are faced with multiple demands on your time, ask, "What is the *one* thing that I must do now?" And then do not let any other tasks crowd it out. In fact, double down on the *one* thing above everything else. Then make yourself make progress.

"IT'S NOT THE RIGHT TIME."

There's certainly something to be said for getting the timing right. Unfortunately, we're not particularly good at judging this in the moment. Often, we don't recognize the perfect moment until it has passed—if there was ever a perfect moment at all. In most situations, conditions will *never* be perfect, so there's no use in waiting, but this is all about procrastination. The saying goes "better late than never," but I sometimes see it as an excuse to settle for later or never. I have an opposite view—in life, it's usually better to be early than late, and that's certainly true when it comes to acting.

A Vice President I worked with at Lehman Brothers in San Francisco used to say, "Why put off until tomorrow what you can do today?" It's a simple, somewhat overused but still powerful question. I have used it numerous times since to give myself an extra push of urgency when I was weighing putting something off until tomorrow. It takes only a second to miss a train that is running on time. Opportunities occur in moments. Practicing courage allows you to maximize rare and valuable windows that present themselves in those opportunities.

"I'LL LET SOMEONE ELSE GO FIRST."

Here's another indicator of an underlying fear of failure. You want to believe that seeing someone else act first will lower the risk somehow or at least help you feel more confident. It probably won't. If they fail, you'll be even more nervous; if they succeed, you'll compare yourself and wonder if you'll measure up. And if you let someone else grab the opportunity at hand, it might turn out to be the only one. Then, when others act and succeed or get glory, will you regret that you had it in your hand and let it slip away? If you're serious about doing something, it makes no sense to put yourself at the back of the line.

A few years ago, there was a viral video going around the internet. I don't know its origin, but it was of a dancing man at a festival of some sort[62] who was bold enough to be the first to start awkward but energetic dance moves that were ultimately joined by everyone on the hill. Most of us don't want to be the first person, but that is what some moments desperately need.

Another way to think about this is: What if everyone is waiting to go second? What if no one goes first? Then no one ever goes.

"I'M NOT THE RIGHT PERSON TO DO THIS."

Maybe you feel like it's not your place. Maybe this action feels too big and daring for you. But who will do it if not you? If you can't point to a specific person, not just someone who *should* do it but who will—the answer is no one. And if you're utterly convinced that you're not the right person, your task becomes to help find the right person and support them in doing what needs to be done. Make no mistake, that is action too.

But again, if you are right there, at the point of action, maybe you are overlooking that you are indeed the right person—the person many, and even you, might have been waiting for. Look no further. Own the moment.

"I'LL TEST THE WATERS BEFORE I DIVE IN."

Sometimes you know a big action is called for, but it's too scary, so you take a half-step toward it instead of going all the way. It seems like a safer bet to do this, but often, it proves to be ineffective. That's because the relationship between effort and results is highly correlated. And when the bare minimum is all you do, you don't see the results. Then you feel discouraged, so you end up abandoning the idea altogether—not realizing that you could have gotten the results you hoped for if you had given it your all in the first place.

Go all in if action is needed. Quit hedging or diluting or watering down the impact that you want to make. Don't get stuck in a self-fulfilling prophecy—a vicious cycle of poor execution that yields no results—and then respond to the bad results with a new narrative to excuse your insufficient action.

"I AM ONLY ONE PERSON."

"There is only so much I can do alone," the excuse goes on to say. Thank goodness the folk heroes in history did not all feel this way, or we would still be stuck somewhere back there. Movements grow and are often inspired by one person or a single action. Don't see yourself as the only person who carries the weight of action but as someone who can be an inspiration to others.

Courage is contagious. It begins close in: one honest conversation, one boundary kept, one person who refuses to look away. You are not responsible for everything, only for the next brave step that is yours to take. Take it, and you will quietly give others permission to take theirs. That is how "only one" becomes many—and how change, the kind that lasts, happens.

As I said before, all these excuses can sometimes be legitimate reasons. The key difference is what you do as a result. When it's an excuse, you absolve yourself, stay paralyzed and do nothing. When it's a reason, you look for ways to resolve that reason—you identify new, intermediate actions to take *now* that will move you toward the bigger action in a concrete way. Don't allow these "reasons" to sabotage your actions and stop you in your tracks.

Don't become an excuse machine and refine the habit of always defending inaction, looking for somewhere external to lay blame, making it others' problem, and absolving yourself of responsibility. Here, there is no learning and no resolve to improve: "I did fine; it was their fault, the rain's fault, my malfunctioning clock's fault."

An alternative approach could be more constructive, focused on understanding what happened, what could have happened differently, and most importantly, how you must act in the future to achieve a more successful outcome. I find it helpful to test my "reasons" against the common excuses. While these can *sometimes* be legitimate reasons, often, they're signs of fear at work.

A few of these saboteurs were at work in my first reaction when I was offered the role in Southeast Asia. My convictions were being tested instantly, and my reaction was to pull back instinctively due to an inexplicable, irrational fear. The prospect of being a brand new General Manager was daunting, even though it had been my desire. I attempted to hide behind the need to think it over a little more. Thankfully, my mentor and my wife gave me the permission to act that I was denying myself. It was indeed the right role for me and the right time for me to be in it. I was the right person for that role at that time. I was to find all this out later. But, if I had walked out of that office without the conversation that we eventually had, the opportunity would have been lost forever, and my life would have taken a different direction. Of that, I am certain.

COURAGE PILGRIM IN ACTION
GARY DESTEFANO (PEOPLE LEADER)

"Be bold."

Nike celebrated its fiftieth anniversary in 2022. The milestone recognized the ubiquitous Swoosh's journey from its beginnings as Blue Ribbon Sports to its evolution into one of the most iconic and culturally influential brands of all time.

Ask a consumer what the brand stands for and most people will say "Just Do It." It is true—Nike relishes action and has inspired us all to get on our feet for decades. Ask a company insider what the company's secret sauce is, and they will point to its people and its culture. This is also true. With successive generations of its innovators just doing it, one of the most impactful brands in the world was created.

Few employees have been in the thick of Nike's mission success or driven its biggest transformational moments as Gary DeStefano. A thirty-year employee who rose to become Nike's number three executive, running all the regions before his retirement in 2013, Gary is one of the company's best leadership exemplars of "Just Do It."

When Nike led the industry in bringing in-house its massively powerful global distributor network, a move that was criticized as risky both for business reasons and its impact on the sales culture, DeStefano led the effort. He accomplished it while revenues continued to grow and with none of the labor fallout that had been predicted. Nike was among the first US companies to establish an owned China subsidiary at a time when there were few precedents for this move. China went on to become the company's second largest consumer market and a key driver of its meteoric growth for over twenty years. DeStefano led that effort as well. For a period in the 1990s, Nike chafed at the way one of its partners was displaying its beloved brand, in misalignment with its standards. Eventually, the company made the dramatic decision to limit products to the retailer, risking significant sales in the process. You guessed it, the issue was resolved, and DeStefano was behind that effort. And when the company kicked off a massive transformation in the mid-2000s, evolving not only its internal brand operating model but also how its retail and wholesale network functioned, ushering an unprecedented decade and a half of industry-leading growth, Gary was one of the key drivers.

I was fortunate to head global market strategy for the company under Gary and to work with him for four years. DeStefano had a keen ability to move through debate and discussion and get to action—when others balked at decision-making, he was clear and resolute. He was part visionary, part business savant and part rebel, and all served him well. But the superpower that made him most magnetic was his ability to take ordinary people and turn them into star actors. He was an astute person whisperer, grounded in the belief that people are at their best when they are building fulfilling lives for themselves, in effect finding their own way. He would encourage us to dream big and muster the confidence to act in pursuit of our dreams. He felt that to get the best out of people, you must respect them as unique individuals with personal stories worth understanding. He encouraged personal mission thinking and, as a mentor and leader, encouraged us to live out our personal missions in our professional work. He would coach gently and ever so firmly nudge you toward action, often toward opportunities he had created for you to shine—like my very first presentation to Nike's Board of Directors. "Be bold," he would say.

At the time, I did not know it, but now I appreciate that not only was DeStefano a meticulous courage pilgrim, but he was also committed to nurturing other pilgrims. Not surprisingly, he was one of the most beloved and effective leaders at Nike, a coach and mentor to generations of managers who now work in leadership roles across the sports and fashion industry and beyond. I asked him what motivated him all those years, and he shared the creed he lives by, "Don't ever forget that you are a citizen of the world, and there are things you can do to lift the human spirit—things that are easy, things that are free, things that you can do every day—civility, respect, kindness, character—that only become real when you act. Actions matter, and results matter. Hold everyone, especially yourself, accountable."

One of my most memorable assignments with him was crafting a $50 billion plan for the company and beginning to lay the foundation for this goal when global sales were still only $15 billion. When we revealed it, the plan was considered breathtakingly audacious, even far-fetched. But it was also very inspirational to the company.

When Nike celebrated its fiftieth anniversary in 2022, both Gary DeStefano and I had long left the company, but I sent him a note, congratulating him when Nike announced that it had surpassed $50 billion in sales.[63] It was a fitting manifestation of his constant counsel to teams and his advocacy for action in service of courage: "The best way to predict the future is to create it."

THE COST OF INACTION

I'd like to dispel a myth about inaction. Some people believe that if they fail to act, the worst thing that could happen is...*nothing*. If there's no action, there's no result to fret about, nothing to regret later. Everything remains unchanged.

But is that true?

Take climate change, for example. Science tells us that it is real and made more severe by human activity. Mitigation is a tough pill to swallow both because of its cost and the requirement that the world collectively makes some urgent lifestyle changes. This will take some effort, and people of the world need some leadership to guide them into making the shift. This means leaders advocating for climate-change action risk being the face of unpopular choices that could cost them politically. One decision could be to act, but the other could be to do nothing and kick the proverbial can down the road. If we continue to choose to do nothing, we'll eventually see that there is not only a cost that comes with inaction but also that the cost can be catastrophically high. Time will tell.

But it's not just climate change—courage impacts the very existence of peace in the world. Martin Niemöller, a German Lutheran pastor who lived through World War II, summed up this truth in a postwar confessional prose about the silence of German intellectuals and clergy during the Nazis' rise to power:

> *First, they came for the socialists, and I did not speak out—*
> *Because I was not a socialist.*
> *Then they came for the trade unionists, and I did not speak out—*
> *Because I was not a trade unionist.*
> *Then they came for the Jews, and I did not speak out—*
> *Because I was not a Jew.*
> *Then they came for me—and there was*
>   *no one left to speak for me.*[64]

I recently visited the Jewish Museum in Berlin and spent several hours one afternoon learning about the decrees, orders, and instructions that Adolf Hitler implemented in the years he was in office. After he became Chancellor, German Jews saw their civil liberties begin to be stripped away, gradually, then at an increasing rate. I was very moved, imagining what it could have been like to feel more and more persecuted by the policies of the Nazi regime with each new pronouncement.

Some families fled Germany, but, as you could imagine, this was not easy to do. Despite their denouncements of Hitler well before the mass murders, many countries did not take significant action to intervene or provide refuge to those being persecuted in the period before the Holocaust—Jewish deaths topped six million. Sadly, the same apathy was replayed in Rwanda in 1994. The international community failed to intervene effectively during the genocide against the Tutsi ethnic group—approximately eight hundred thousand people lost their lives.[65]

In both cases, those who could have acted earlier equivocated, hesitated, and stalled. I am sure that lots of explanations and reasons can be offered for inaction, but the bottom line is simple. A few lacked the courage to act, and as a result, millions of lives were lost. Sadly, there are way too many stories like this throughout history.

The same hesitation that allows injustice to spread on a global scale can also quietly undermine progress in a company—missed decisions, delayed innovations, and unchallenged poor behavior often start with business leaders convincing themselves it's "not the right time" to act. Kodak and the digital camera,[66] Nokia and the smartphone shift,[67] Uber and workplace culture issues,[68] Boeing and the 737 MAX crisis,[69] and Facebook/Meta and misinformation all come to mind.[70]

Inaction is seldom beneficial—it only promotes at least one of the following consequences.

PERPETUATION OF FEAR

One common consequence of choosing not to act is the perpetuation of fear. If fear is the reason we avoid acting in the first place, that decision only allows our fear to grow, unchecked and uncontested. Inaction could raise the stakes of risk, erode our credibility, and make fear a bigger factor down the road. For example, an understandable and harmless fear of speaking in public when we are in college could grow to become quite debilitating and negatively consequential when we are a thirty-five-year-old Sales Manager who needs to present to clients.

Modern psychologists understand the value of exposure therapy, the practice of exposing patients to their fears so that they can form new opinions about the true dangers involved. In other words, it could take *action* to change your feelings about something.[71]

PERPETUATION OF THE STATUS QUO

While inaction along your personal journey perpetuates fear, inaction in a social context perpetuates a status quo. And what if the status quo is deterioration? Or physical harm to others? Or an abusive relationship? Or a bad job situation? Should it be allowed to remain in place through inaction?

In 1987, as AIDS hit US front pages but remained poorly understood, fear filled the gaps—many believed any contact could transmit the disease. Months into this climate, the late Princess Diana sponsored an AIDS ward at London's Middlesex Hospital and, before the press, deliberately shook a patient's hand without gloves. That simple act challenged and widely dispelled the myth of transmission through casual touch. Had she recoiled, the panic would likely have deepened; instead, her compassion shifted the public conversation.[72]

As this story illustrates, even the smallest action can have an enormous impact. Life is a complex mix of dynamics, interactions, and influences—a bit like a chemical reaction. Sometimes, adding just a tiny amount of something different can change the outcome entirely and give rise to new possibilities that others can build on. Just take Rosa Parks' famous decision to challenge the status quo by not giving up her seat on a Montgomery, Alabama, bus. This seemingly small action catalyzed the Civil Rights movement and propelled Dr. Martin Luther King, Jr., to prominence, not to mention inspiring thousands of others to act as well.

MISSING THE CRUCIAL TIME WINDOW

Another consequence of choosing not to act is underestimating the true value of timing. Sometimes, the opportunity to act is a rare one, or a limited one. Missing a window of opportunity could mean letting a magical moment pass you by, never to return.

On Saturday, February 1, 2003, Space Shuttle Columbia disintegrated as it reentered the atmosphere over Texas and Louisiana, killing all seven astronauts on board.[73] During the launch on January 16, a piece of insulating foam broke off from the shuttle's external tank and struck the thermal protection system tiles on the orbiter's left wing, setting off a chain reaction that led to the tragedy. What is not as widely known is that mission staff on the ground debated not only what had happened but what to do about it for two weeks. Ultimately, they did nothing, and the shuttle was allowed to make its return voyage to earth.[74] Upon re-entry, it exploded, not only killing the crew but adding to a growing drumbeat for NASA to discontinue the program, which it did, in 2011. So, yes, inaction could have a huge, irreversible cost.[75]

Again, choosing not to act is an act in itself. So, yes, if you're experiencing sleepless nights when you are avoiding taking action on something, that's for good reason. It means that the status quo needs to change, you are running out of time, and in the interim, someone is being negatively impacted. To come back to the scope of this book, that someone is likely *you*. You may not even understand the negative impacts to your physical, mental, and emotional well-being by not acting when you should. But apathy and indecision are creating unease in the background—gnawing at your sense of peace.

Beware of the power of moments when action matters the most. And remember that if something needs to change, then an action needs to occur, and someone must take it. Be comfortable being that person and be courageous enough to do something about it. Otherwise, you could be numbing yourself to opportunity or lending your precious voice to legitimizing or normalizing an undesirable status quo.

Although most of us will never face decisions with stakes as high as war, genocide, or corporate collapse, the courage to act—or the failure to do so—still defines our impact in the arenas we do inhabit, whether in leadership, community, or personal life.

We'd like to imagine that if we don't act on things, conditions will simply stay the same, waiting patiently for us to do something someday. But conditions around and within us are constantly changing. Inaction is a form of action, just not the type of action that I am prescribing here. I dare say there is no such thing as a neutral position. Neutral is where fugitives from courage go to hide when they would rather not act. Neutral is capitulation looking for a fig leaf. We talked earlier about how courage is a virtue that seeks the common good. How can neutrality coexist with a claim to courage?

PRIME FOR ACTION: READINESS CHECKLIST

In addition to being honest with ourselves about our excuses and being aware of the consequences of inaction, there are many things we can do to prime ourselves for action. We don't have to do all of them all the time. But the more we practice these things, the easier it will be to choose courageous actions when the opportunity arises.

FOCUS ON YOUR PURPOSE

Moving halfway across the world to take a job in Malaysia was a huge decision, but I made it in an instant and executed it within days. Notwithstanding my initial hesitation, how was I able to say "yes" and act so quickly? My story earlier could make it seem like I was dragged into action. Not quite.

It goes back to the clarity of *purpose* we talked about in Chapter 2. When I was offered the Southeast Asia position, I already knew my long-term goals and my short-term needs—I was looking for change, seeking a challenge, and hoping to take on a new type of leadership role—specifically general management in a local market. I had given myself a timeline to transition by year-end.

When I realized that the new job fit all my criteria (in a quick instant and with that little nudge from my mentor and support from my wife), I found the courage to say *yes*. So it was not an answer completely out of nowhere. It was not impulsive.

But here is one thing. I hesitated…why? Because of ego. Should I, as a direct report into an influential C-suite leader, not naturally shift into a large sexy market, in Europe for example? Should I take a "step down" into a small market? Again, I was faced with a choice: respond with my ego or listen to my sense of purpose and my heart.

If we know exactly what we're striving for over the long term, it will be easier to weigh new opportunities against that purpose in the short term. At first, this analysis happens on an intellectual level—it's a conscious thought process that you undertake deliberately. But the more deeply we understand and identify with our purpose, the stronger our intuition around it becomes. We'll start to recognize instantly, at a gut level, whether an opportunity serves our purpose or not. In this case, guts overcame ego. So allow yourself to trust that gut feeling, and it will grow even stronger over time and guide you. That's how you'll be able to act quickly and with confidence, even when you first hesitate or when the stakes are high—like moving your family across the globe!

KEEP AN OPEN MIND

Even with a clear purpose, courage often requires us to notice opportunities we didn't expect—and sometimes, those opportunities look nothing like what we first imagined.

Another lesson of my Malaysia experience is how it helps to reframe how one looks at opportunity. The only way we know how to do things is *not* the only way they can be done. In fact, as Thomas Jefferson put it, "If you want something you've never had, you must be willing to do something you've never done."

An enormous number of growth opportunities existed at Nike, but most of them were not in the US or Europe. I knew that there were fewer open roles in these large markets and that I had fixated on them perhaps too long and lost sight of the exciting opportunities available in other places. In a way, defaulting to inaction and frustration. That is, until I was reminded how my blinders were on a bit too tight, narrowing my focus in many ways.

Being courageous is about being creative. Sometimes that means doing the surprising or the unexpected. It comes down to what we need on our journey and aligning that need with the right opportunity, which may not be in our normal line of sight. In fact, it often won't be. As flight attendants say on planes, "Note that the nearest exit may be *behind* you."

SIMPLIFY YOUR DECISION-MAKING

Before you act, you must decide what action to take. It's easy to get hung up on this step—laying out the options, doing research, asking other people's opinions, and generally wallowing in information without making any progress. We stay stuck because we're "figuring it out" with likely too much data and information (it's often another excuse). That's why it's crucial to develop a simple, reliable way to make decisions.

There are two keys to this process: (1) defining your parameters and (2) prioritizing them. By parameters, I mean the factors that influence your decision. For example, if you're buying a house, there are a lot of factors that might be important to you—the price, the size, the number of bedrooms and bathrooms, the condition of the house, the location, the proximity to schools or public transportation, etc. It's often useful to brainstorm a big, comprehensive list of all the things that matter.

However, those factors are not all equally important, which is where prioritization comes in. What is a must-have versus a nice-to-have? If you must choose between two things, say, square footage or location—which matters more to you? Of the dozens of parameters that you brainstormed earlier, you will probably find that only a handful are truly determining factors in your decision. One or two may even be nonnegotiable. This massively simplifies your decision process because it means you can minimize, if not ignore, all the other stuff and just focus on your top priorities.

You don't always have to make decisions like this. When your intuition gives you a strong gut feeling about what to do, consider that too. But when you're stalled at this stage, approaching the decision in this systematic way could help you get moving again.

DECIPHER TIME-BOUND ACTIONS

Once your options are clear, the next question is "when." Timing can amplify the impact of a courageous choice—or erode it, as we described before in the Space Shuttle Columbia reference.

In the business world where everything is dynamic and information is always changing, the heroes of the moment are not always the most knowledgeable people but often those who own the moment. We can all point to incidents where one person just said or did the right thing at the right time and seemed to drive an organization one way or the other with astute placement of themselves. Even more noteworthy, I am sure there might have been times when you had the instinct to do or say the exact same thing, but you hesitated—and watched someone else seize the moment. To work on your timing, all you might need to do is stop second-guessing yourself so much and hesitate less.

Default to action. Plant a stake on the calendar and challenge yourself to deliver in full, on time, and as promised. Strive for excellence but remember that excellence also lives within constraints, including time constraints.

PRACTICE SAYING YES

The easiest way to get better at seizing the right moment is to make action a habit—by saying "yes" more often. By this I don't mean going for any and everything, willy-nilly. My point is to see action as a muscle. The more you use it, the easier it gets. So, if you want to be ready for action when big opportunities arise, practice saying "yes" a little more. Start with saying "yes" to small opportunities.

Practice builds skills, confidence, and intuition in a low-pressure way so that when the stakes are high, it's easier to go for it. This is what athletes do so that on game day, their actions are second nature. The most legendary athletes—Simone Biles and Serena Williams—are renowned for the work they put into practice. Thus, they can make an impossible play look easy when they're on TV and the entire world is watching.

Keep your eyes open for chances to practice saying "yes" and act when you normally might sit back. In a group meeting, when the leader asks everyone to introduce themselves, volunteer to go first. At the end, when they ask who will take responsibility for some action item, raise your hand. When your daughter asks if you can build a treehouse, instead of putting it on your project to-do list, go to the hardware store *that day*. Whenever you can do something small that's aligned with your purpose, do it immediately, without hesitation.

What you'll learn is that most of the time, you don't *really* need to think about it or put it off until later. Plus, each small action contributes a little to an overall sense of progress and fulfillment in your life. Practice consistently and you'll look back on your week or month surprised at how much you got done—even if not perfectly—how much good it generated, and how many new opportunities arose because of those small actions.

DO YOUR PREP WORK

Of course, saying "yes" without preparation can backfire. Courage isn't recklessness—it's informed readiness for the opportunities you choose. You've probably heard the adage that luck is what happens when opportunity means preparation. When you know a big opportunity for action is coming up, it pays to make sure you're as ready as possible to take courageous action.

Recently, I joined the Board of Directors of a nonprofit organization, which was stacked with strong executive leaders with decades of diverse experience and impeccable credentials. It's an exciting honor to join a group like that, and initially, it was a little nerve-racking as well. Instead of wallowing in this feeling, I handled my anxiety in a different way—I prepared. By my first meeting, I had done my homework on every member and spoke with each one. When we convened, it wasn't a room of strangers. We'll talk more about this in Chapter 8 when we discuss the difference between self-worth and self-confidence and the role that preparation and experience plays in our ability to grow self-confidence.

CREATE BREATHING SPACE FOR YOURSELF

Thoughtful action takes preparation. Preparation takes bandwidth. When your calendar is crammed, you rob yourself of the mental space needed to act with intention in high-stakes moments. Space allows for reflection too—each experience carries lessons that sharpen your judgment for the next challenge.

Busyness is the default for many, but constant motion is often just an excuse that undermines courage. If a critical meeting is wedged between urgent tasks, you'll arrive frazzled instead of focused. Whether it's speaking up for yourself, advocating for others, or navigating a hard conversation, courage thrives in a mind that's calm and ready—not one that's scrambling to catch up.

Part of ensuring you'll act when it counts is protecting your bandwidth. That might mean arriving early, rehearsing key points, or walking in with possible action scenarios and letting the facts guide you toward the right one. This is preparation without impulsiveness.

Think like an athlete in training: training blends effort, recovery, and rest because self-care fuels performance. The same principle applies to courage—you need intentional pauses, mental recovery, and deliberate practice. Without space to breathe, you can't summon your best self to act confidently when it matters most. We'll touch on self-care a little more in Chapter 8.

COURAGEOUS ACTION IS NOT RASH

As we consider the power of action, I must acknowledge that much has been written about the action fallacy, the mistaken belief that doing something—anything—is inherently better than doing nothing, especially in moments of uncertainty, crisis, or discomfort. This type of action is often driven by impulse, the illusion of control, avoidance of helplessness, and social pressure, essentially the performative motivations that do not define true courage.

This is not the type of action that I am advocating for. Courage is thoughtful. I recall Aristotle's caution quoted earlier in this book—that courage falls on a spectrum between cowardice and rashness—what Aristotle called the "Golden Mean." If inaction and doing nothing sit on one end of the action spectrum, poorly considered action and impulsive action sit on the other end of it.

Acting with courage is an entirely different thing, as the writers about the action fallacy rightfully call out. Recognizing the action fallacy is crucial for thoughtful decision-making. True, sometimes, the most courageous or strategic move is *not* to act immediately—but to pause, reflect, and choose deliberately.

That said, once deliberations have been completed, the need to progress and act decisively is both a critical and an important choice in the courage journey that cannot be overstated.

ACTION BRINGS NEW PERSPECTIVE

Now that you know how to prime yourself for action, there's one more crucial reason to act, even when the cost of inaction seems low or the potential gains seem minimal. With every action you take, your perspective changes. I often think of this in terms of rock climbing, which I used to enjoy doing when I was much lighter and nimbler. Each move revealed new holds. Action changed what I could see and what was possible—the same is true in life. Action brings new perspectives that make progress easier. The key is to get started by placing the first foot forward.

Revisiting my move to Southeast Asia is a fitting example of how I expanded my perspective on my career. After my "spur-of-the-moment" decision to take the Nike job in Malaysia, we ended up staying in Southeast Asia for almost three years, and it was one of the best professional experiences I ever had. There was a dual opportunity to help craft, lead, and oversee both a region and country in transformation. I was invaluable to the market as a former architect of the company's global strategy. I gained valuable sales, brand management, general management, and people management experience that has served me well in the years since. I caught the international bug and progressed to become an expert on growing consumer brands around the world. I would have missed that opportunity—and all the ones that followed—if I hadn't been pushed to act at once in that office.

While this is one example, among many, of me taking courageous action in an important life decision, there were also many moments when I sat back and let the opportunity to act pass me by, only to regret it later. Actions do not always yield desired results, but my summation, from my experience, is that a strong bias toward action is infinitely preferable to none.

FINAL WORDS—STEP INTO THE ARENA

The wrong choice is to fail to follow through—to stay on the sidelines, endlessly preparing, planning, or waiting for the perfect moment. That choice leaves your potential locked inside, your purpose unfulfilled, and your courage untested. True growth comes only when you step forward and act. Action is what separates dreaming from experience. You can't simply read about courage or imagine it into existence—you must practice it in motion. As Theodore Roosevelt reminded us in his famous words, it is not the critic who counts, nor the one who points out how the strong man stumbles, but the man in the arena whose face is marred by dust and sweat and blood. The credit belongs to the one who dares to step into the fray.

To live courageously, you must claim that arena for yourself. No one else will swoop in to rescue you from inaction. It is your responsibility to chase your aspirations, set new goals, and create momentum even when the next step feels small. Every decision to act, however modest, brings your purpose to life and builds the resilience you need to move forward.

And if you wonder whether your actions are the right ones, remember this: if they move you closer to your goals and align with a noble purpose, they are enough. Because the real question is not whether you will fail—it's how you respond when you do. Next, in Chapter 7, we normalize the stumble—how to metabolize failure without losing speed.

A CALL TO ACTION: MASTER THE FIRST STEP

Action is the bridge between courage as an idea and courage as a lived reality. It's where resistance gathers, hesitation hardens, and excuses multiply. The first step is often the hardest because it demands the most thrust—like a rocket breaking free from Earth's gravitational pull; you must generate your own escape velocity to move forward.

THE GOAL OF THIS CALL TO ACTION

To build a bias toward taking the first step—creating momentum that overcomes hesitation and reduces the cost of inaction.

HOW TO BRING IT TO LIFE

1. **Set clear deadlines and commit to them:** A defined timeline puts healthy pressure on you to start, leaving less room for procrastination.
2. **Create social accountability:** Share your goals and timelines with your inner circle so they can challenge hesitation and encourage follow-through.
3. **Break goals into small steps:** Even daunting goals are made up of manageable moves. Focus on one step at a time to reduce overwhelm while still making progress.
4. **Act before you feel "ready":** Perfection is a moving target. Start with what you know now—momentum will expand your capacity.
5. **Practice saying "yes" more often:** Build your action muscle with small, low-risk opportunities so it's easier to move when the stakes are higher.

KEY ENABLERS OR CHALLENGES TO BE MINDFUL OF

- **Deadlines without accountability can still slip:** Pair them with trusted voices who will hold you to your word.
- **Waiting for certainty often means missing the window of opportunity:** Timing matters, and sometimes prompt action is the only action that counts.
- **A small, imperfect action is usually better than no action at all:** It creates learning, momentum, and new possibilities.

Momentum is born from movement, not from waiting for the perfect plan. Commit to the smallest, clearest action you can take now—and let that first step open the path for the ones that follow.

CHAPTER 7

GROW FROM FAILURE

"Success is not final; failure is not fatal: it is the courage to continue that counts."

—WINSTON S. CHURCHILL

In 1983, I remember making a deliberate choice to avoid failure for the first time.

I was eleven years old, standing on the starting line for a race at my primary school's annual sports day. Our entire school, roughly three hundred school children, staff, and tons of parents and family, was present. Us kids, waiting for our chance to participate in different events, sat under four large thatched huts on one length of the dusty field, mere feet from the freshly lined track. Directly opposite sat guests. There was a huddle of people near the finish line, positioned to cheer and get great photos of the young athletes. My parents were there too.

The 4x100 m relay was one of the most anticipated races of the meet, and the four starters for each team were taking their places on the track. I was one of them. I had run this race before but never started—that was an honor reserved for the top athletes—and after two years of running in this relay, I knew that I was a decent competitor at best. But I had run so well in the practice meet the week before that our house coach had switched me from the third leg to the first. Now, my teammates were relying on me to explode out of the blocks and set us up for victory with an early lead.

As we lined up, I checked out the other kids. They were among the fastest in the school. I gradually became concerned, then convinced, then alarmed that I would not hold my own with them. I envisioned myself coming in dead last as everyone—my parents, classmates, and hundreds of strangers—looked on. The more I thought about it, the more I worked myself up. Before long, my heart began to pound. My breathing became shallow. My muscles tensed. My hands became clammy and started to shake. I felt sick to my stomach. I thought I was dying. That didn't help.

As the official conducted the final check, the runners on either side of me stretched and bounced, getting ready to give the race their all. Not me. I was frozen in place. A parent who was volunteering stopped the official and pointed at me. "Wait, I think this kid is sick," he said.

The official walked over and crouched to peer into my face. I tried to pull myself together, but my lungs couldn't seem to get enough air, and my fingers wouldn't release their grip on the bottom edge of my shorts. I was gasping, hyperventilating like crazy.

"He's not sick," the official said. "He's just scared." He peered into my eyes. "Do you want to go back to the hut?" he asked me.

Before I could even wrap my mind around that idea, my head was nodding. The official stepped back, and I felt the hand of the chaperone on my shoulder, guiding me to the sidelines. As he beckoned to the coach, who sent another boy out onto the track to replace me, a wave of relief rolled over me, and I slowly relaxed. That evening, my mom gently asked, "Why didn't you run your race?" Today, I don't remember what I told her. But I remember that it was not my finest moment.

Churchill's words remind us that courage isn't a onetime act—it's a sustained practice of moving forward, even when the last outcome didn't go your way.

Looking back, I wish the official or parent chaperone had patted me on my back, assured me that I would be fine, and let me run. Who knows how I would have done? I could have led the pack and realized that I have a running talent that could have shaped my life differently. I could have ruined the relay for my team and felt embarrassed, but that would not have been a death knell. The truth is it would have done me well to lose the race. I hadn't failed *enough* in life.

I chose this early story deliberately. By eleven, constant wins had become part of my identity—ace in class, even tying for first nationwide in secondary school entrance exams—so even small losses felt like threats. To protect the image, I avoided risk and, in the process, starved the courage muscle. That warped calculus—100 percent success, 0 percent failure—became a weak link in my journey for years, keeping me from trying, speaking up, and making bold calls. I'm a much different person as an adult, but I don't want those early habits for any part of your life: failure isn't a verdict; it's the workout that builds perspective, resolve, and opportunity—and without it, you miss both growth and moments you can't get back.

OUR ANTI-FAILURE REFLEX

Google the word "fail," and you'll instantly be flooded with stories, headlines, and video compilations of people's worst moments packaged as entertainment for some or as dire warnings to the rest of us. Watch the news and see how quickly the reaction to mishap turns to "Whose fault was it?" or "When will they resign or be indicted, sued, or canceled?" The message is clear—in society, failure is *not* a good thing, and it is something we have been conditioned to think must be avoided at all costs. The consequences of failing are, at worst, severe and, at best, the source of ridicule and scorn.

This view is sneakily pervasive, and when you take a closer look at what our culture praises and what it criticizes, it's easy to understand why. Adoration goes to those who get the best results—the valedictorian, the best-selling author, the unicorn founder. In virtually every sphere of life, lackluster results get you ignored, punished, or rejected. We don't know how to talk about or celebrate those who are not first or the best, and we do our utmost to conceal our own failures—the shortcomings of our imperfect selves.

Sometimes, we even snicker or laugh at others' failures—setting ourselves up to keep ours forever hidden from sight or to pretend that we have none. Even in everyday interactions like dinner with friends, there is this undertone of judgement and one-upmanship—a constant comparison of who has the better edge. We don't seem able to resist posturing and presenting ourselves as flawless.

The crazy thing is that we all fail all the time; it's just that we are trained to mask it and pretend that we are incapable of failing, if not habitually perfect. After all, results do matter in life. *But when you look at it this way, is it any wonder that we go to great lengths to avoid failure?* Inwardly we know the truth, but we hold others to these unfair standards all the time. It feels like an insidious game, one that we could lose ourselves in, and many indeed do. Somewhere at the intersection of Fear Street and Failure Avenue is where many souls on the journey of courage meet their demise.

We praise outcomes over process, so we hide stumbles and equate mistakes with shame. That conditioning makes risk feel expensive. In a recorded-by-default world, even minor missteps can feel career-defining, and we self-censor. But the more we hide failure, the less we practice recovery—and recovery is where learning and courage are built.

WHAT KIDS CAN TEACH US

The fact is that no one is born with a fear of failure. A toddler who is learning to walk doesn't see a fall as failure. They run into tables and walls with absolutely no shame. All day long, they stand and fall, stand and fall. They get frustrated, of course, but they recover quickly and try to stand again. They keep trying until they get it right, blissfully unaware, and they couldn't care less about what anyone else thinks about their attempts. Eventually they master walking and go on to running or pole vaulting or even mountain climbing. They progress.

But as we grow up, we're continually judged by our results, and we hear and sense this response around us. Parents, teachers, coaches, and classmates praise us for our successes and purse their lips at our failures. It isn't always extreme or even intentional, but it's there nonetheless. And the older I got, the more I cared about what other people thought of me and the scarier the prospect of failure became.

Now, as a parent of two preteens, I have an entirely new perspective. Through their tablets and phones, kids have endless opportunities to compare themselves to others and find ways to feel inadequate. At the same time, they're more sheltered than ever, with less unsupervised free time than previous generations. Parents feel an obligation to protect their kids from experiencing too much failure and from real life's missteps and recovery.

All of this is a perfect recipe for *true failure*—the state where you are too fearful to fall, too sheltered to grow, and too stunted in developing courage to live your authentic life. Unless you are lucky enough to grow up surrounded by people who continually praise your *efforts at the process of discovery and learning*—not just your results—you probably know this fear. When we encounter a challenge that might result in failure, we're hesitant to even try. We experience self-doubt and walk away from the opportunity, telling ourselves that it is simply too difficult. Sometimes, we try to reassure ourselves by pretending that we don't really want the reward on the other side of the hurdle. "It's just not for me" or "The time was not right," we tell ourselves.

This view of challenges as win-lose propositions, as opportunities to be either a hero or an embarrassment, is a limiting mindset. It tells us that failure is evidence that we're not capable of attaining our goal, that we're not good enough and might never be. But there's a different way to think about failure—one that will push you toward a courageous life instead of holding you back from one.

FAILURE MAKES US STRONGER

By teaching us humility and perseverance, and offering invaluable lessons that success often overlooks, failure undoubtedly makes us stronger. When we fail, we are forced to confront our weaknesses, adapt to new challenges, and develop problem-solving skills. Each setback provides an opportunity to learn, grow, and improve. By experiencing failure, we gain a deeper understanding of both our capabilities and our limitations, which in turn helps us to approach future challenges with greater confidence and insight. Additionally, there are three primary problems with attempting to avoid failure.

1. INNOVATION REQUIRES ITERATION

Failure is a fact of life; you will experience it at some point, guaranteed. And if you haven't had much practice at dealing with it before it happens, that failure will be devastating. It will feel like the end of the world.

In contrast, when you allow yourself to experience many small failures, you learn how to cope with them. You get good at picking yourself up and dusting yourself off. The sting no longer hurts badly. And instead of viewing failures as losses, you learn to see them as feedback; each one is another piece of information guiding you to success.

In 2011, Netflix launched a major change: separating its DVD-by-mail business into a new brand called "Qwikster" while focusing its core offering on streaming. The move backfired spectacularly—customers hated the split and confused pricing, and the shift disrupted the brand's simplicity, leading to subscriber losses and a significant stock decline.[76]

Instead of doubling down, Netflix reversed course—abandoning Qwikster, issuing a public apology, and refocusing on an integrated user experience. This demonstrated humility and resilience in the face of failure. This failure did not stop the company from growing into a global media powerhouse, generating billions in revenue, and leading the industry it helped create.

2. FAILURE BUILDS CHARACTER

The second problem with avoiding failure is that it also means avoiding opportunity. The two go together—every opportunity also comes with a risk that things will not go your way. Each risk also comes with a commensurate reward. If you focus on avoiding those risks, you'll miss crucial chances to pursue your life's purpose and fulfill your personal potential.

Stephen King, the master of horror, began submitting short stories to magazines at age twelve. Shortly thereafter, he received his first official rejection, an impersonal form letter from *Alfred Hitchcock's Mystery Magazine*. If King had been worried about avoiding failure, he would have quit at once. Instead, he took that rejection notice, speared it with a nail over his bureau, and kept submitting his short stories to various publications. After a couple of years of submissions, that nail "would no longer support the weight of the rejection slips impaled upon it." So what did the young Stephen

King do? He "replaced the nail with a spike and went on writing." No doubt becoming a better writer at each turn.[77]

We've already discussed many examples in this book—of bounce backs after initial failures, the critical point being that failure brings learning and imparts wisdom and perspective that positions us better for the next opportunity.

3. AVOIDANCE TRAINS STAGNATION

The third problem is the more you avoid failure, the more skilled you get at failing to grow. Yes, you read that right—the more you avoid failing, the more skilled you get at *true failure*, the state where you are too fearful to fall, too sheltered to grow, and too stunted in developing courage. The key is to see the avoidance of failure as the version of failure that must be avoided. Even though it may be tempting to see it as a success of sorts—you avoided the pain of failure—you also side-stepped the opportunity to grow and got stuck on the path to mediocrity.

When I was in Malaysia, I heard a captivating speaker on the radio one evening as I drove home from work. My team needed a shot of inspiration, so I called him up and invited him to take us through one of his workshops. I remember the first thing he said to us—failure is a skill. For a moment, we recoiled, but I knew immediately that he was right! Just as we might build expertise at something by putting in time into it, we stay bad at something when we keep avoiding chances to fix it. In other words, the more we avoid failure and don't enjoy its positive impact, the more we get skilled at not growing and continue failing. In other words, we lock in stagnation.

COURAGE PILGRIM IN ACTION
SIMIDELE ADEAGBO (OLYMPIAN)

"I am not expecting to be perfect, but I am committed to doing my best."

Simidele Adeagbo's Wikipedia profile reads that "she retired from Track and Field competition in June 2008" after "she failed to qualify for the Olympics by eight inches" in the triple jump event.[78]

Simi describes the aftermath of missing her Olympic dream "as a dark transition period," a phrase which captures her remarkable story eloquently. It took some time, but Adeagbo picked herself up from the darkness and disappointment and decided to rewrite the rest of her story. She did not retire from her ambition but instead transitioned from the "empty" feeling of 2008 to become Nigeria's first winter Olympian and the first Black female Olympian in the sport of skeleton.

Adeagbo's journey is a tale of self-motivation and rediscovery. A four-time NCAA All-American and triple jump record holder at the University of Kentucky, after her 2008 near miss, she shifted focus back to her Nike product merchandizing career. Seeking deeper fulfillment in her role, she moved to Nike's Johannesburg office, where working on the South Africa FIFA World Cup campaign ignited her passion for inspiring African youth through sports.

Determined to pursue her Olympic dream, Adeagbo learned in 2016 about Nigeria's bobsled team, reached out to the team, and subsequently placed into skeleton. Just one hundred days after starting the sport, she competed at the 2018 Winter Olympics in Pyeongchang, South Korea, becoming the first Nigerian to participate in the Winter Games. She finished twentieth in skeleton, a feat she applauded herself for, and proudly served as Nigeria's flag bearer at the closing ceremonies.

Her path continued to be anything but easy. Living in her mom's house in Houston, Texas, there was no track to train on. Nigeria had no heritage in winter sports and no money for the skeleton startup team. She had no coach, no equipment, and no advocacy when global rules tried to muscle her out of competing. She took to paid motivational speaking to fund her way and supplement her modest Nike sponsorship. When she attended competitions, she had to endure the looks, snickers, and sentiments that said, "You don't deserve to be here. You don't belong here." Most times, she was alone; her family was supportive but could not always afford to travel. By then, Simi knew that the fairy tale was not hers but belonged to thousands of young people, especially girls, who were cheering her on.

She experienced moments of doubt and would ask herself why she was doing this, but she drew on her failure in 2008 to be thankful that she had nothing left to lose. The dream was too precious to quit. She adopted her own mantra, "I'm strong. I'm powerful. I'm fast. I'm born to do this."

In 2022, Simi took first place in the women's monobob event in the Europe Cup in Winterberg, Germany, becoming the first athlete from Africa to win an international sled race.

Simi is living her dream of making a difference. An ambassador for the Malala Fund and a member of the Obama Foundation Leaders inaugural class, she has spoken at events like TEDx and Forbes Women's Summit and appeared in *USA Today*, *Essence*, and *Forbes*. In 2021, she founded the Simi Sleighs Foundation to support marginalized female athletes and empower girls through sports. A year later, she authored her first children's book, *Sleigh, Sleigh, Sleigh All Day*, and credits the messages in it to the lessons of her failed 2008 Olympics bid. She teaches her immense following of school-age girls around the world to not regard failure as a reason to give up.

Simi's win in Winterberg was a moment of vindication for years of failure and recovery. It might have surprised many, but she says she always knew that day would come. She wrote on her Instagram: "With personal best down, and push start times, I raced for an unprecedented feat and earned a decisive victory. Some didn't expect to see an African woman atop the podium. In fact, there was no Nigerian flag or anthem on hand for the awards ceremony. No matter how unexpected my victory may have been for some, it was a shining moment in which my dream became a reality."

Adeagbo, forty-four, is not done. At writing, she is training hard with the goal of securing a spot representing Nigeria in the two-woman bobsled competition at the 2026 Olympic Winter Games in Milano Cortina, Italy.

Individual lives aside, I have seen these three problems occur in corporate cultures as well. Some companies are risk averse. They penalize those who try to be creative and try new things that they label "disruptive" or "misaligned." These companies tend to get bogged down in "old think" and "no think." They rationalize and embrace the unpleasant habits as "our culture" and purge anyone who dares to challenge it. Often, they spiral downward. Does this hit close to home?

Other companies might embrace ideas, newness, and change. They are invariably the ones with strong, innovative cultures, more growth, and more satisfied employees. They develop a culture of success, as opposed to an institutional skill of failing.

Simply, we'll get much farther in life by embracing failure than by avoiding it. But to do so, we need to learn how to spot our own tendencies that can make it harder to do this work.

OBSTACLES TO EMBRACING FAILURE

While failure can, in fact, make us stronger, we all have personal tendencies and obstacles that can conspire against us in this effort, specifically, perfectionism, a negative environment, playing only to our strengths, and viewing vulnerability as a weakness.

PERFECTIONISM

Some of us develop a penchant for perfection (guilty as charged). If this is you, you probably already know it. You're a stickler for rules and details. Good never feels like enough; you want everything to be *exactly right*. You sweat the small stuff that others don't seem to notice. You tinker and refine for *ages* before you feel ready to share your work. Sometimes, you would rather do nothing than do something that does not meet your standards.

You take pride in your perfectionism—I sure used to. I wore it as a badge of honor. On the inside, I looked down on others who were unable or just didn't care enough to set the bar as high as I did. The academic world rewarded me for this way of thinking with high grades and honors. It was a huge asset when I started my career on Wall Street too, where missed details and miscalculations could destroy millions or billions of dollars in massive transactions.

But I soon learned that in much of the business world, and in life at large, the obsession with perfectionism can be a liability. This is particularly true in today's rapidly changing climate. Some industries, like high tech, evolve so quickly that by the time you perfect a new product, it no longer has a place in the world. Beta products are released quickly to the public to gain market share and increase consumer loyalty (and over time, with feedback, firms work out the kinks and bugs in them). The faster you introduce something, the sooner you get reactions from real customers, who guide you in the right direction and keep you from wasting time on the wrong path.

In Harvard Business School's high-intensity case-study teaching and learning culture, by the time you craft the perfect thing to say, the conversation would have moved on, fueled by someone else's timelier, even if less sophisticated, insight. I found this out the hard way. As an executive, taking too much time to overanalyze a decision could leave your team disoriented and listless, and your senior leaders concluding that you are indecisive and not up to the job. Because tastes and trends change constantly, perfectionism can cause you to be left behind.

Even nature itself does not worship at the altar of perfection as we do. Those rows of perfectly round apples and perfectly yellow bananas in the grocery store? Nature didn't do that. Nature produces plenty of lopsided, undersized, twisted, and generally knurly looking fruit (which you'll find if you go to a local farmer's stall, like the ones I used to shop at in the wet markets of Freetown, Port Louis, Kuala Lumpur, and Denver). That "ugly" fruit is delicious, but big chain grocery stores won't stock them because they don't meet corporate and consumer standards of perfection, or the appearance of one.

Perfection simply isn't natural. In fact, it can be wasteful, inefficient, and suboptimal. Being human means making mistakes; it means failing. So why do we chase perfection so obsessively?

In the end, seeking perfection is just another way of hiding from failure. It's a misguided attempt to be *sure* that when we finally share whatever we've been working on, it will be received with praise and not criticism or ridicule. It's ego protection cleverly disguised as "high standards."

So, whenever you find yourself getting upset over minor flaws or holding back from sharing your work, pause and recalibrate. Move the bar from "perfect" to "good enough." Pursue a process of continuous improvement and make progress. Challenge yourself to share your ideas and work as you go along so you can get feedback and learn from it. Some of that feedback might not be what you're hoping to hear, but it's much better to fail quickly and correct a course early than to wait until after you have devoted too much time and resources to being perfect and lost other opportunities to grow and be better along the way.

PLAY TO POSSIBILITIES (NOT JUST TO STRENGTHS)

When I mentor folks, I try to learn as much about them as I can. I get to know their strengths and weaknesses, and I work to identify critical gaps in their knowledge or experience that they can address as a growth opportunity. When we spot an area of weakness, I usually suggest that they tackle a challenge to improve that skill. Unfortunately, sometimes, my advice is turned aside. "I think I should rather play to my strengths," I have had people tell me. I've even had employees turn down promotions because they felt the new roles I offered them didn't align with their strengths—even though they were actively seeking out more responsibility and growth.

Someone (even with the best of intentions) may have advised you to "play to your strengths." It makes sense that you should highlight or leverage what you already do quite well and let it continue to form positive impressions of your abilities, doesn't it? But this strategy will eventually leave you with glaring unaddressed deficiencies. As you pursue a fulfilling life—one with meaning beyond yourself, you may need different skills at various points in your journey. At one time or another, you may need to manage, sell, negotiate, give service, create, nurture, stand up for your beliefs, or compromise. To get closer to your purpose, you'll need to fill in the gaps in your own skillset. If you don't do this, your courage journey could be slowed when critical abilities are missing at opportune times, so be aware that you are a work in progress.

In these ways, we don't want to simply stick with our strengths all the time or choose only roles or organizations where we're not challenged. Instead, we want to leverage our strengths and *play to possibilities*. Try new things. Develop new talents. Get out of our comfort zones because discomfort is where growth happens. If we play to our strengths, we have a high probability of short-term success. But if we play to possibilities, we have a higher probability of long-term growth. The courage to develop new skills often comes with the discomfort of looking inexperienced—and that's the point. Every stretch role, every attempt at something new, will carry the risk of not looking like the expert you are in other areas. But that very discomfort is the training ground where courage grows and where long-term growth outpaces short-term success.

I know that looking at our weaknesses and pushing beyond our comfort zones can be scary. If you have anxiety about entering new environments, consider moving in adjacencies, where you have one foot firmly planted in your strengths while you explore with the other foot. When I left investment banking and joined Gap, I did so in the treasury department, where I could leverage my strengths in corporate finance and strategy while learning about the lifestyle fashion industry, which was new to me. Eventually, once I had learned much more about the fashion business, I transitioned from a finance role to working in brand strategy. This experience made it easy to then shift into a key business unit strategy role at Nike, leveraging what I had learned about brand strategy at Gap. Once at Nike, I shifted from strategy to sales and from US-based roles to international roles, driving transformation and reporting into the C-suite, leading to living as an expat for over a decade. You get the point. You can take chances and make dramatic changes while keeping one foot on solid ground, your strength. Don't let the risk of failure stop you from growing and learning and taking on brand-new challenges.

ENVIRONMENTS THAT PUNISH LEARNING

Just as children can be made to feel shame or embarrassment after failure, adults can also be affected by the judgment of others. If you have worked hard to master a healthy mindset toward failure, but you're surrounded by colleagues who view failure differently, you may have a challenging time maintaining your progress. It's important to avoid negative or judgmental environments.

So look around you. What's the prevailing attitude toward failure among the people you spend the most time with? Do they embrace failure, or do they only applaud success? When failure happens, do they seek to learn from it, or are they more concerned with assigning blame? Who succeeds in the organization where you work and who gets promoted? Those who toe the line and parrot the status quo or the risk-takers who look for new opportunities for the organization?

Sometimes, an anti-failure culture is obvious: rewards are tied only to results, not effort or progress. Those who succeed are showered with praise, while those who make mistakes are criticized, rejected, or ignored. When failures happen, everyone rushes to cover their butts and point their finger at someone else—it's more important to identify *who* caused the failure than *why* it happened or *what* to do about it or *how* to grow from it. An environment like this will only amplify your fear of failure. Moreover, it is not a place that's conducive to much learning.

Anti-failure attitudes can be subtle too. Supportive colleagues might say things like, "It's okay, we all screw up sometimes. We're here for you." Comments like this seem nice, but they frame your single attempt as a "screwup," instead of one step in a longer process.

In an environment that truly embraces failure, folks understand that failure isn't the end of anything. It's a routine part of doing business. When failure happens in an environment where leaders encourage their team to grow from failure, people will say, "Good job—we now know what doesn't work, and we learned a lot from your attempt. Could you document your learning? Thank you!"

A few years ago, when my wife and I read bedtime stories to our two children, one of the titles they both loved was *Beautiful Oops!* by Barney Saltzberg, a playful guide for turning mistakes into new possibilities.[79] Unsurprisingly, it was Daddy's favorite book too. As a person who built a career driving business transformation, an aversion to failure would have limited my impact. I have walked away from failure-averse companies—more than once. In fact, I relish situations where failure is believed to be imminent, and I have built a career proving these are instead growth opportunities.

VULNERABILITY IS A PERFORMANCE ADVANTAGE

How often have you heard "Fake it till you make it"? Once, an executive teammate wore that mantra like a badge. Confidence in uncertainty matters—but only when it's matched by the work you are putting in to improve. He was more *fake* than *make*: polished in meetings, light on substance, and a weak link when the team needed execution. You've met people like this. I reject the mantra. It licenses concealment—hide the gaps, varnish the results, spin a story. That isn't courage; it's pretense. Courage names the gap, does the reps, asks for help, and takes on the challenge. Confidence is acting while learning; pretense is acting without learning.

But you might be thinking, isn't it important to stay positive and put on a bright face to encourage and build confidence for us and our teams? Yes, good leaders know how to be encouraging and inspire confidence, but they do so without creating false narratives. They are still honest in focusing on growth. The risk here is that we might begin to believe our own false narratives, forget the need to work on our development, or, worse still, lead others astray with our false bravado.

To truly embrace courage, we need to do the opposite; we must first accept vulnerability. Only through exposing ourselves to the possibility of failure can we truly practice the skill of courage. By stepping into situations where success is not guaranteed, we expand the boundaries of our comfort zones and allow for personal growth. Placing ourselves in an intimidating scenario, where criticism and rejection are very real possibilities, exemplifies the courageous vulnerability required to innovate and lead.

Vulnerability in the context of courage also means being open to learning and being transparent about our shortcomings. Consider a manager who recognizes that they lack certain skills needed to effectively lead their team. Instead of hiding this weakness, they openly discuss it with their team and empower members to shore up where they are weak, not only building mutual trust and confidence within others but also preparing them for leadership.

In this way, vulnerability opens us to receiving help and improving ourselves. It humanizes us and helps us connect better with others. Vulnerability makes us more honest with ourselves and others, less choreographed and more confident. If we don't locate our vulnerable selves, we cannot locate courage. I have witnessed this firsthand.

In 2005, Nike's top US leaders gathered for an annual offsite in Kauai, Hawaii. I remember the opening night vividly. The theme was "What's your 10/2?" inspired by Lance Armstrong's revelation that October 2 was the day he was diagnosed with cancer. (Armstrong had been a Nike athlete prior to his doping scandal.) The goal was for all of us to reflect on the most transformational event of our lives, and a small handful of people got up on stage to present their stories. Each one was a powerful disclosure of a personal struggle of overcoming adversity. None was a glossy story about personal heroism or a sunny narrative about faking their abilities while trying to make it. Each leader served up a raw, honest, and vulnerable look at themselves in that transformational moment, and there was not a dry eye in the room.

Miraculously, the entire event shifted in purpose and feel in the days after. We grew closer together and appreciated the humanity in each other as we shared our 10/2 stories in smaller groups. Consequently, we saw our personal growth stories as fuel for larger possibilities. When we eventually got to strategic planning for the region, the team worked even better together, visioning and delivering another run of the massive growth the brand was known for. Ultimately, it is this depth of vulnerability that makes the difference when you need to connect with your inner core, your inner strength—to pick yourself up after a setback, find your courage, and do something big with your life.

FINAL WORDS—FAIL, LEARN, CONTINUE.

The wrong choice when failure arrives is to unravel with setbacks—to allow disappointment to define you and keep you from trying again. Failure is never the end of the story unless you decide to stop writing it. The courageous path is to accept failure as a natural part of the process, a teacher that sharpens your perspective and strengthens your resolve. Each setback is not a verdict against you but an invitation to adjust, grow, and keep moving.

Fulfilled people are not those who sidestep failure; they are the ones who face it, learn from it, and rise again. They treat failure as feedback, not finality. When you can view failure as routine—simply a way to eliminate wrong answers—you remove its power to paralyze. Over time, you may even welcome failure for the insights it brings, knowing that each stumble positions you closer to your purpose. This mindset liberates you from the grip of fear and keeps you on course.

Of course, the journey is not without effort. Courage is a lifelong pilgrimage, and while it demands persistence, it is not meant to be a weary toil. There will be high points and hard days, seasons of momentum and seasons of setbacks. What matters most is not avoiding the struggle but staying committed to the path.

And that commitment requires resilience. To sustain your pursuit of a courageous life, you must care for your mind, body, and spirit. The energy to rise from failure repeatedly comes from cultivating strength and joy within yourself. That is where we now turn in Chapter 8, our final choice: the practice of embodying resilience and joy as the enduring foundation of courage.

A CALL TO ACTION: SEEK PROGRESS OVER PERFECTION

Failure is not a judge—it's a teacher. When we obsess over perfection, we raise the stakes so high that failure feels catastrophic and progress stalls. But courage grows when we shift our focus from flawless outcomes to steady, deliberate improvement. Progress is within our control; perfection is not.

THE GOAL OF THIS CALL TO ACTION

To replace perfectionism with a mindset that values learning, iteration, and visible progress—reducing fear of failure and increasing your capacity for courageous action.

HOW TO BRING IT TO LIFE

1. **Reflect after every setback:** Ask: What worked? What didn't? What can I do differently next time?
2. **Track learning, not just wins:** Keep a log of experiments, lessons, and adjustments—evidence that you're moving forward, even when results aren't perfect.
3. **Share your failures with trusted voices:** Talking about missteps reduces shame, invites fresh perspective, and normalizes risk-taking.
4. **Reframe success as progress:** Celebrate steps taken, skills gained, and resilience built—not just final outcomes.
5. **Challenge your perfection triggers:** Notice when you're delaying action to "get it just right" and instead move forward with what you have.

KEY ENABLERS OR CHALLENGES TO BE MINDFUL OF

- **Private versus public growth:** Public outcomes get more attention, but the private process shapes the real growth—don't ignore it.
- **How you feel versus what is observed:** Social embarrassment is often imagined and rarely as damaging as we fear.
- **Continuing unmaking fear:** Seeking perfection can mask fear; try to identify what you are fearful of.

Perfection will always be a distant or elusive target—but progress is a finish line you can cross every day. Keep stepping forward and let each imperfect attempt build the courage and skill that perfection could never teach you.

CHAPTER 8

EMBODY RESILIENCE (AND JOY)

"Everything can be taken from a man but one thing: the last of the human freedoms—to choose one's attitude in any given set of circumstances, to choose one's own way."

—VIKTOR E. FRANKL

By now, you get the message. Courage is a journey. It is built over time through ordinary decisions, against adversity, and with steady steps that compound into meaningful change. Choosing to start the journey shows commitment; choosing to weather the journey is resilience. In practice, resilience is how purpose survives contact with time, pressure, and setbacks. It is the sustaining choice that keeps courage operational after the first surge of momentum fades.

Our earlier chapters introduced the choices that accelerate courage—commit to a purpose, own your potential, act decisively—and the choices that help manage its decelerators—unmask fear, and when headwinds are strong, reject distracting voices, grow from failure. Resilience plays a different role. It is the sustainer that keeps us through all of it. It preserves our drive when the scoreboard is not favorable, and it converts hardship and lessons into better judgment and resolve rather than into hesitation and surrender.

The figures mentioned throughout this book were not defined by a single instance of valor. Abraham Lincoln's impact emerged through iteration under pressure. Nelson Mandela's commitment to purpose did not shrink to the size of his jail cell; it clarified and deepened. Harriet Tubman and Dr. Martin Luther King, Jr., both advanced their missions through cycles of advance, resistance, reassessment, and renewed commitment. The common denominator is continuity—staying with the work long enough for aligned actions to compound.

We have also discussed courage as personal and situational, meaning each of us will require resilience but not in identical ways. But, as this book has posited, we all need to be vigilant and self-aware on two fronts, on which our courage will be contested.

- **Internal limits:** Resilience is required *to confront and replace self-limiting beliefs*, to move forward despite internal doubt, and to translate insight into the next concrete step.
- **External constraints:** Resilience is required *to withstand bias, noise, and opposition*, to keep standards and voice intact, and to act in alignment even when the environment penalizes it.

Seen through Frankl's lens, both modes represent that "last human freedom." This is the role of resilience in a courageous life: to sustain the choice of one's way—not once but for as long as the mission requires.

RESILIENCE IN ADVERSITY

While writing this book, I spoke with a long-time friend, a successful venture capitalist in Silicon Valley. I respect him for his success and for his breadth of perspective. Over Thanksgiving dinner at his home, our conversation turned to the role courage had played in our lives. I shared my view of courage as a superpower available to anyone who seeks to leave a mark or to build a better life.

He was skeptical about who can truly be courageous. His argument was that courage is contextual—shaped by circumstances, as I would agree.

He went on. If you are battling inequity or systemic bias, as he had as an immigrant to the United States, risking the little you have can feel like a luxury you cannot afford. And for those for whom survival is on the line, purpose can seem secondary, and courage could be risky.

The implication matters. If courage were contingent on perfect conditions, only a narrow slice of people would ever qualify for the pursuit of purpose that required risk-taking. This book takes a different position: that circumstances influence the *cost* of courageous action, not its *possibility* or its *criticality*. Courage is not gated by status. It is available to all of us, and resilience—applied to our specific constraints, internal or external—is what enables that possibility and converts it tangibly into a fulfilled life.

That said, the cost of courage is undeniably higher for some facing some disadvantages, which is precisely another reason resilience matters. By some, I speak of those who don't feel included or who are targeted for their difference, especially those with inimical differences—the newcomer, the woman, the LGBTQ person, the person from the other side of the tracks, the person of color, the person from another country, etc.

WHEN YOU HAVE NOTHING TO LOSE

Joan of Arc was a *peasant girl* who found martyrdom and sainthood when she was pronounced guilty of witchcraft and burned at the stake in 1431 at the age of nineteen. Her crime—a girl leading French forces against the English occupation.

The diminutive Mohandas K. Gandhi *faced the might* of the British Empire as he led the independence movement for India, organizing mass protests, boycotts, and the famous Salt March, all of which were met with harsh reprisals from British authorities.

Mohamed Bouazizi was a Tunisian *street vendor* who set himself on fire on December 17, 2010, in the town of Sidi Bouzid. This act was in protest of the confiscation of his goods and the harassment and humiliation he endured at the hands of local officials. It became a catalyst for the Tunisian Revolution and the wider Arab Spring, a series of anti-incumbent uprisings across the Middle East and North Africa.

Among the legions of civil rights activists who changed the course of US history, most were not particularly wealthy or privileged. Many were not politically powerful, but they did what they did anyway. And many were "different" from the groups they were opposed too.

They all faced the cost of their actions—some paid with their lives—but they refused to let their resolve be reduced by the forces arrayed against them. And they left us all better off.

Some might call these people exceptions to the rule, but I don't think so. What I take away is that courage is often born from frustration with the status quo. Courage is the difference-maker for the better life that is desired.

In our own everyday lives, the stakes might not be as high, but our calling to courage is the same. Especially when the odds seem stacked against us.

AN ALTERNATIVE NARRATIVE TO VICTIMHOOD

I am no folk hero, but I have faced situations where I felt helpless and powerless, and I know how this assails the very notion, if not the practice, of courage itself. I know how it feels to be intimidated by an abusive and oppressive power, having lived through a dictatorship in my childhood and having experienced discrimination in my adult life, including as a professional. Unfortunately, far too many people around the world have *only* known situations like this, or far worse, in their lifetime. Far too many people are victims of circumstance and birth and must navigate life from a place of disadvantage. Notwithstanding this, courage is a lifeline for them too.

I first felt that helplessness on a sunny afternoon in 1987. I was sixteen, and walking home from school, when I came upon a traffic jam near the turn onto our street. It was clear that there was a car crash ahead. A passerby mentioned mangled cars, unknown casualties, and a brown automobile. I froze—the only brown car in our neighborhood was my father's vintage Hillman Hunter. On instinct, I ran to the intersection and pushed through the crowd that was gathering.

Three vehicles were scattered across the road. Two were red Toyota Land Cruisers—government issues for Cabinet Ministers and members of parliament—each crushed on one side. My father's car was worse: both flanks crumpled, the chrome bumper twisted into a V, the engine block dropped to the pavement, oil pooling beneath. It looked unsurvivable. Yet my father stood beside it, dazed and silent. When I reached him, he murmured my name, then sank to the ground, breathing heavily, as if my arrival gave him permission to let go.

When the police arrived, witnesses described what happened. My father had slowed, signaled left—with the indicator and his arm, as he always did—and began his turn toward our street. Two Land Cruisers packed with schoolchildren tried to overtake him simultaneously, one on the left and one on the right shoulder. The first struck the left side of his car and spun it 180 degrees into the path of the second, which hit and spun it back. The other two drivers had been racing.

A neighbor drove my father to the hospital; miraculously, he was physically fine. Back at the scene, the children from the red vehicles were quickly collected and taken away. My mom arrived from her work, and we waited for the police.

About an hour later, a black Mercedes sedan bearing the national pennant arrived. Officers snapped to attention. A tall, impeccably dressed man stepped out, surveyed the wreckage, and asked where his children were. Told they'd been sent home safely, he turned to leave. He glanced toward us. My mother stepped forward—"I am the wife of the driver of the brown car..."—but he looked past her, said nothing, got into the back of the Mercedes, and departed. It was my first and only encounter with Sierra Leone's Vice President, Attorney General, and Minister of Justice.

It was a crushing feeling, on one hand, witnessing my dad's narrow brush with a tragic end and, on the other hand, my mom's advocacy for him and our family's loss disregarded. My experience with that government official was a shock to that idealistic kid, and it left me reeling with confusion and a sense of humiliation—of being devalued and cast away. I certainly did not feel capable of courage at that moment and certainly not in the face of someone so powerful. On the contrary, I felt, well, quite small. We were ordinary citizens living under an autocratic regime where incidents like this were unfortunately quite common, constantly reminding everyone of the political and social hierarchy in the country and our relative places in it. But we qualified as middle class. What of the families who were more economically disadvantaged?

I am using this example to make an extremely broad point—that some of us will find ourselves in temporary or permanent situations where we are at a disadvantage within an environment, not seeming to "hold the cards," so to speak. We might be at the receiving end of those who hold a stronger hand and who wield that hand firmly for themselves or against us. In these cases, the quest for courage should not diminish. I argue that it should be more urgent.

COURAGE STANDING UP TO POWER

When put-downs, beatdowns, and battering happen consistently to a person or group, they harbor more discomfiture and self-doubt. And we know by now that self-doubt erodes courage. Yet, there is a crucial point to understand. Just because someone is "under attack" does not mean they can no longer practice courage. It simply means that it may be harder to do so. The truth is that as much as we feel disempowered, courage is the best tool with which to fight back. Hope is not lost.

If I had been brought up to believe that courage was a luxury reserved for people like that man in the suit, I might have let that feeling of powerlessness sink in. It might have taken root under my skin and become a permanent fixture of my existence and of how I saw myself relative to the established power structure at home. I would see myself as helpless and hopeless. There would be no reason to write this chapter, maybe even this book. But courage needs no permission, and it is yours to wield. Courage is your own superpower with which you can confront many challenges.

I remember sitting next to the driver of the tow truck who hauled our car away. With nowhere else to take it, we left it in the front yard of our rented flat, where it stayed for years, a stark and persistent reminder of our family's lack of power. We could never afford a replacement car, nor did the government ever compensate my dad, apologize, or acknowledge the accident. Our family walked and rode public buses after that.

Nonetheless, at the same time, this incident left me with a piercing demonstration example of my parents' dignity. Where I was angry and hurt, they were grateful that our family was safe. While that day was certainly one of the most egregious incidents of injustice in their lives, they were not deterred from their purpose to be good parents of well-adjusted children. Instead, they responded with resolve to harness and manage what they *could* control—resilience to overcome the odds, an unwavering devotion to fairness and integrity, and their unquestionable commitment to giving us kids the best lives they could.

Thanks to their example, I learned that there is an alternative to seeing myself as a victim—angry, subdued, or otherwise. I didn't call it courage at the time, and neither did my parents. That day changed my understanding of power and justice, but my parents refused to let it reduce our belief in our own dignity. It deepened my understanding of self-control and self-worth.

ANCHORING RESILIENCE: SELF-WORTH AND SELF-CONFIDENCE

Since this chapter will discuss how to endure the courage pilgrimage with resilience, I wanted to dwell a little longer on what I learned from my parents' reaction to my dad's car accident.

Without question, the incident left me flirting with self-doubt, just as I was approaching adulthood. It rattled my parents too, I could tell, but while their confidence was shaken briefly, their sense of self-worth remained secure. We developed this model in Chapter 3, and it is worth repeating: self-worth and self-confidence are critical for courage and keep resilience, the sustainer choice, from collapsing under strain.

Patrice Evra is regarded as one of the best left-backs to have played professional soccer. Among others, he played for the English club Manchester United and the France national team, where he served as captain. Born in Senegal, he moved to France as a child and overcame significant poverty to become a professional footballer. Evra made the news often for the relentless racism he suffered during his playing years. He recently shared about his experiences on one of his social media accounts:

> People used to make monkey noises at me during football matches. And it used to throw me off my game early in my career. Later on I realized that I couldn't control people. I could only control how I reacted to them. When you react badly, they win. When you lose control, you lose power. When you let their words in, you give away your strength. So I focused on playing the game. I smiled. I won. True power is keeping your focus when others try to break it. Be selective about what you allow into your mind. That's how you win the real game. If you let words control your emotions, you'll always be controlled by others.

Notwithstanding his unpleasant experiences, Evra became a highly decorated player, winning five Premier League titles and a Champions League trophy with Manchester United. After a stellar playing career, Evra is now a successful entrepreneur, motivational speaker, and social media personality with his "I Love This Game" brand. Another positive outcome, yes, but clearly a sometimes-bumpy ride.

Do you have a powerful sense of self-worth, or is self-confidence something you lack, or vice versa? Understanding the two and working on them becomes part of the process of building courage.

Self-worth is your deep belief in your inherent value—the conviction that you matter, regardless of what you achieve or how others treat you. Self-confidence is your trust in your ability to perform a specific task or handle a particular situation. Resilience is the capacity to recover and keep going when things don't go as planned.

Self-worth is the foundation; self-confidence is the structure you build on top of it; resilience is the reinforcement that keeps the structure standing through storms. You build self-worth by grounding yourself in your values, practicing self-compassion, and surrounding yourself with people who affirm your dignity. You build self-confidence through preparation, practice, skill-building, and by taking small, consistent actions that prove you can follow through. And you build resilience by learning from setbacks, applying those lessons forward, and refusing to let adversity define you.

One is who you *are*, one is what you believe you can *do*, and one is how you *keep going when tested*—and courage thrives when all three are strong. I have tried to cover all these dynamics in this book. They are all important for this journey. As I shared early in the chapter, building resilience is about vigilance and self-awareness on two fronts—internal and external; Both are immensely critical for success.

COURAGE PILGRIM IN ACTION
WENDY LEA (SYSTEM BUILDER)

"I took the worst of times and turned them into lessons that I can draw from."

In 2020, during the COVID-19 pandemic, the State of Colorado launched the Energize Colorado initiative to address the economic impact on Colorado's seven hundred thousand small businesses. Wendy Lea, then sixty-six, was tapped to lead the ambitious project to foster a resilient and equitable small business ecosystem at a time when small firms the world over were stumbling and shuttering.

Wendy's forty-year career cements her reputation as an "entrepreneur extraordinaire," known for tackling complex challenges and driving innovation in urban systems. Her journey spans roles as a corporate executive, strategist, angel investor, and Board Director. But what Wendy sees herself as is an ecosystem builder. She founded TechHubNow! and earned recognition as a Silicon Valley Woman of Influence, a P&G Signal Excellence Award honoree, and a University of Cincinnati Distinguished Service Award recipient before leading Energize Colorado. It was at Energize Colorado that I first met Wendy when I served as a volunteer mentor to small business owners.

Wendy is no stranger to complex challenges and attention-grabbing success. She came to Colorado fresh from creating a business ecosystem for the city of Cincinnati and, before that, experienced the painful failure of a startup she ran in Northern California. She is the first person to admit that her superpower is not her business acumen or her people skills or even her ability to collaborate, even though all are stellar. She is clear that it is her resilience—not only her commitment to continuous learning and growing but also her ability to emerge energized from misfortune and mishap.

Lea muses that her resilience comes from growing up the first of four children born to a seventeen-year-old mother in rural Mississippi. She thinks some of it could have come from her Buddhist mother's take-it-in approach to life, which contrasted starkly, if lovingly, with her own lifelong go-getter approach and a burning ambition to be an entrepreneur and make a substantial impact. She also credits her gift of self-awareness, which has injected reflection, purpose, and intention into all that she does.

No matter its source, Wendy's resilience was put to the test on one unforgettable morning in February 1976. The twenty-seven-year-old was at home enjoying the weekend after a grueling week at her corporate job, catching up on chores at the home she shared with her husband. He was a student in medical school and had once been her high school sweetheart. The phone rang, and suddenly she was down at the local morgue identifying Robbie. All but one person in a jeep that was bringing him back from a fishing trip had been killed in a tragic rollover. Wendy was devastated. As if that was not enough, her three-month-old niece died of spina bifida shortly after. And around the same time, her dad, a pillar in her life, was diagnosed with terminal leukemia and died in her arms at the age of fifty.

Wendy's experience with sadness, grief, despair, doubt, uncertainty, and fear has known no bounds, but rather than stop her, the death of loved ones motivated her to strive even harder for her goals, recognizing how fleeting life can be. She describes the tragedies as triggers to her resilience and her immense sense of responsibility to achieve her potential as a human being. When you meet her, sadness is not what you sense—joy and exuberance is what you feel.

At seventy, Wendy continues to raise her hand for more challenges. As I was interviewing her for this book, she was named one of Colorado's Top 25 Most Powerful Women in Business. Her years have convinced her that the most effective leaders are those who have had to bounce back from severe challenges and lead with more heart. And for her part, her way of healing is to be resilient, and her approach to resilience is to keep moving forward with a relentless focus on creating positive change in the world.

NAVIGATING ADVERSITY

But how—how does resilience sustain us? I found in my interviews that there are many paths and approaches to consider and to follow here, but I did want to share some that I and some others use.

FACING REALITY

I had to confront the issue of racism early in my professional career when I was in my twenties. As an international student from Sierra Leone, I had not been familiar with the experience of discrimination before I moved to the US. However, my Morehouse experience forewarned and prepared me, so when I eventually started encountering race dynamics at work, I was not totally caught off guard.

Discrimination is a tough wall to hit and even more insidious when it is based on something inimical. Our reactions to it vary. Some spiral into shock, confusion, and self-pity and get bogged down lamenting how unfair the experience is. They are thrown off the real work that needs to be done—recovering and coming back strong. A talented college schoolmate of mine was accepted into medical school and promptly had some experiences that he felt were discriminatory. He would spend hours recounting to us how other students in his class were treated differently and more fairly. He was rattled by what was happening to him and could not move on past it. Ultimately, he dropped out of his program and never became a doctor.

Being courageous is about being deliberate about your choices, and being realistic makes a difference in how you grow in courage. My son is a mixed-race teenager, raised with love, but that will not shield him from having to confront the harsh reality of being a male of color. He is smart and well-traveled and well-read. Some people will conjure him as everything but what he really is. They will choose not to see the gentle soul that he is and the loving family that raised him. I know I must sit him down and tell him about the realities he faces. As a parent, I feel terrible having to take away his innocence in this way, especially since many of his other friends don't have to have these conversations at his age. Is it fair? Absolutely not. But for him to navigate life more intentionally and stay in control of his choices, he needs to be clear-eyed about the tough reality to come.

This is critical for him if he is to experience discrimination and not let it derail him from the path to his purpose.

It is no different for some of you. Anticipate that there will be obstacles in your way. Take that as a given and train yourself not to be thrown off your game.

GROWING A THICK SKIN

Over the years, I have also learned to pick my battles, knowing what to react to and what to ignore.

Not too long ago, we were visiting my in-laws in Cheyenne, Wyoming, and I was out running errands with my wife's dad. We stopped at a gas station, and while he sat in the passenger seat of my car, I got out to pump the fuel. Suddenly, out of nowhere, an elderly woman pulled up to the pump next to mine, got out of her car, took one look at me, and yelled, "Nigger!" She followed it with an expletive-laden rant about me going back to my country before she got back in her vehicle and sped off without even buying gas.

In fifty years, it was the first time in my life I had been called *nigger* to my face, but I was oddly unconcerned. Instead, I thought, "I hope you find peace from whatever pain you are feeling." I did not even mention it to my father-in-law, who was unaware of the incident and would have been distressed on my behalf. Yes, for a split second, I was indignant and had an impulse to lash out with my own expletives, as my much younger self might have. Instead, I felt sorry for her.

If I reacted to every offensive word, slight, and act of aggression toward me, real or perceived, that's all I would have time for all day long. You have learned by now that courage needs focus, and I cannot cede my focus, time, or emotional energy to just anyone, certainly not strangers who have no consequence in my life. A random woman in a random gas station spewing hate does not make the cut as deserving of *my* time.

Embodying resilience is about staying in the game long enough to score big points and not losing sight of the prize. Don't empower anyone to disempower you.

BEING YOU AND STAYING YOU...UNAPOLOGETICALLY

What is unique about each of us is what makes us interesting to others and valuable to society. It is what helps us see the world in a different light and solve problems more innovatively. It is what inherently builds upon our authentic selves and creates a stronger platform for self-belief, confidence, and courage.

It's not always comfortable to be someone who stands out, but this is not a weakness; it is a strength. You'll need to come to terms with this. I had to get over that a long time ago because I am often the only person of color in many places where I find myself professionally. I grew to appreciate why it is an asset. Sometimes, it lures people in like bait during cocktail hour. They want to know who I am, how I got into the room, and what my story is. I am never offended. Often, it leads to interesting conversations, great networking, lots of learning, and even new friendships. "You are intriguing," someone once said after an in-depth exchange, and he was being sincere.

But as I said, it will not always be construed in a good way. Your difference could be weaponized against you. It will happen. But know and remember this: your difference is a strength, not a liability. Diversity is productive and sustaining—ask any biologist, economist, or anyone who has a responsibility to study systems that drive innovation. This includes human and cultural diversity, which over centuries powered art and science and civilizations. To argue against these facts is simply preposterous. So be proud of the diversity that you represent. It is an asset—don't let anyone make you believe otherwise.

WORKING HARDER THAN EVERYONE ELSE

Researchers have found ample evidence that those who hail from certain underrepresented groups must work harder and be better to earn the same breaks as others.[80] Sadly, some of us can relate to this—that overexcelling is part of the preparation necessary when your credentials are likely to be questioned or scrutinized. I would not say that I face disadvantage everywhere I find myself, but I do know that working harder than others are willing to do has been a key success factor for me. Often, it is a necessary door opener and often the minimum prerequisite to receive earned recognition. It is also how I stay in control of my own narrative—it's a little harder for someone to recast me in theirs when I outperform and outmatch them on substantive objective measures. More importantly, it boosts my self-confidence and, ultimately, courage.

When I joined Nike from Gap in 2005, I was appointed to a highly desired role—one that had attracted numerous talented internal candidates. I knew this and wondered why the position had been offered to me, an outsider, when there was such a deep and qualified pool of internal talent interested in the opportunity. Someone who had been on the interview panel confided in me later, "It was one of the most desired jobs in the company, but you stood out from the entire pack not only because you were so well-qualified but also because you came in so prepared and extremely confident and self-assured. You knew things about the company that many of us in the room did not know. There was no way we could go with someone else." The habit of doing things at a higher level of excellence compared to everyone else is what sometimes provides that differentiating margin that earns you a seat at the table. I know it might seem like an unfair burden to carry, but, as I said at the start of this chapter, that's why we are talking about resilience.

As I have shared before, though, this can be a double-edged sword. Needing to over-excel just to be gain access to some opportunities can lead to an obsession with perfection or self-imposed standards that are so high and unrealistic that you get in your own way. It can lead to stress and ill-health—physical and mental. Both are unfortunate hazards to be aware of and manage (I'll say more about this shortly).

INVITING YOURSELF IN

It may surprise you to learn that I didn't and don't have life passes or standing invitations into the hallowed halls of opportunity. I don't have a presumptive right to access any place. But, at the same time, being courageous also means not always waiting for an invitation. Over time, instead of expecting to be invited, I got used to inviting myself into places and situations. I don't mean barging in and gatecrashing. I mean leaning into opportunity and not shutting doors for myself that no one has shut on their own. I am an advocate for showing up, and unless someone stops me at the door or tells me not to, I walk in as if I belong. Rather than disqualify myself based on an imagined constraint, I think, "What is the worst that can happen? I get turned away? I can survive that!"

For the past few years, I have been building a corporate governance career. It's a challenging aspiration, as only a handful of board roles come open each year, and most of them are filled from within the network of existing board members—in other words, networking is key. Networking for corporate board roles has required a strategic and intentional approach—one that goes beyond my traditional circles and into the spaces where potential sponsors spend their time. Since most boards are still dominated by sitting or former CEOs and CFOs, most over the age of sixty-five, this means showing up where they convene: industry conferences, philanthropic galas, alumni events, and exclusive leadership forums, where I can build necessary relationships. When I asked for advice from one of my friends who sits on a Fortune 100 board, she said that one of the things she did (and still does) is push herself to just show up. She seeks out and accepts invitations to be in places where her network can grow, no matter how intimidating or awkward it feels. She recognizes that every handshake and every conversation opens possibilities for new connections, and the more she allows herself to be seen and known, the easier it is for new boards to imagine her at their table. She is not just simply sitting at home, waiting for the phone to ring. Even after all her success as a former Fortune 100 Chief Financial Officer, she understands the need to take these small proactive actions and make them second nature. As I do. As can you.

WALKING AWAY

Back in Chapter 5, I said sometimes quitting is for winners. I quit roles when the negative pressure was too much and all options I pursued to create a positive and productive environment for myself had been exhausted. We are all programmed from an early age to find virtue in remaining dogged and not quitting. Like most people, I share this belief, but in the pursuit of your best life, quitting is sometimes the right move. To live a life without regrets, it's critical to know when to walk away.

In 2005, at the height of his career with *Chappelle's Show*—a cultural phenomenon in the US—comedian Dave Chappelle walked away from a $50 million contract with Comedy Central. In the middle of filming its third season, he decided he didn't like the direction the show was taking, nor the environment it was creating for him. So he left. Just like that.

Many saw it as career suicide. But Chappelle later described it as a decision to protect his integrity and his well-being. More than a decade later, he returned to stand-up comedy on his own terms, releasing a series of hit specials on Netflix. He regained not only his audience but his voice—stronger than before.

Sometimes resilience looks like staying the course through adversity. Other times, it's having the courage to walk away when the cost of staying is too high.

Did I leave some good places where I enjoyed working? You bet.

Did I walk away from specific situations that were not in my best long-term interests? Always.

Did I learn from these situations? Every single one of them.

Do I have any regrets? None. Better opportunities came along. We owe ourselves that.

It's not quitting when you make a choice for more opportunity, more respect, more recognition of your worth. You are simply deciding to deploy your time and resources somewhere else, where you are more valued and where you can live the life to which you are entitled. It's not quitting when you are making a bigger bet on yourself. There is no shame in that—you are living life on your terms.

TOXIC RESILIENCE

In one of my interviews for this book, I was introduced to the concept of *toxic resilience*—the shadow side of grit—the kind that keeps you pushing through adversity while quietly eroding your well-being. It's when the drive to "bounce back" becomes compulsive, self-neglecting, and even harmful.

This is not what I call resilience, because resilience is sustaining and thriving. Still, it is important to acknowledge that this is what many see as their only coping option. Resilience is not just about gritting your teeth and pushing through. It's about making sure the body and mind that must carry you are strong enough for the journey. Self-care, mindfulness, and tending to your mental health are not luxuries; they are essential. Courage needs clarity, and clarity comes from a mind that is rested, grounded, and able to think beyond the noise of the moment.

For me, that has meant carving out space to be still—whether through solitude, quiet reflection, walking in nature, or simply stepping away from the constant pull of emails and alerts. It has meant carving time with loved ones who accept and value you unconditionally. It has meant listening when my body says *enough for today* and respecting that limit without guilt. And it has meant knowing when to ask for help—whether from my inner circle or others—because going alone isn't proof of strength; it's often a recipe for burnout.

Resilience isn't pretending you're unaffected or passively accepting every slight that seeks to undermine you. Resilience is being thoughtful about how you can be active, being strategic about the qualities you can deploy and how best to expend your energy as you stay on the path of building courage. Resilience is biding your time as you weather rough patches so that you can continue toward your purpose.

It's exactly what Dave Chappelle did—stop making others laugh so that you can laugh later louder for yourself.

WELCOME IN, JOY

In 2022, Ketanji Brown Jackson became the first Black woman and the first former federal public defender to serve on the Supreme Court of the United States. Judge Jackson graduated from Harvard College, then attended Harvard Law School, where she was the editor of the Harvard Law Review. She had more years of experience as a trial court judge than any Supreme Court justice in history, in fact, more than four of the sitting justices in her cohort combined. She served on the influential United States Court of Appeals for the District of Columbia Circuit. The American Bar Association rated her as "well-qualified" (its highest rating) to serve on the US Supreme Court. She was a candidate with exceptional credentials, unimpeachable character, and unwavering dedication to the rule of law. She was hailed for her record as a jurist and regarded by all who knew her as an objective and courageous advocate for fairness and justice.[81]

And yet the Senate Judiciary Committee put her through twenty-two grueling hours of questioning in which numerous attempts were made to besmirch her credentials, her record, her judgment, her integrity, and her self-worth. Superfluous questions about every decision she had ever made seemed designed to throw her off balance and distract the public from her impressive narrative. It was hard to watch. But she did not break or give in to indignation and anger that would in turn have been used to undermine her candidacy further. Toward the end of the hearing, Senator Cory Booker of New Jersey expressed what many of her admirers and supporters were feeling:

> You have sat with grit and grace and have shown us just extraordinary demeanor during the times where people were saying things to you that are out of the norm…And you did not get there because of some left-wing agenda. You didn't get here 'cause of some dark money groups. You got here how every Black woman in America who has gotten anywhere has done: by being like Ginger Rogers said, 'I did everything Fred Astaire did but backwards in heels.' And so I'm just sitting here saying nobody's stealing my joy, nobody's going to make me angry…[82]

It was an experience that had been anything but joyful, so Mr. Booker's emotions and choice of words were notable. As much as the moment called for resilience, for him it also required a need to remain optimistic and cling to joy.

THE WAY OF JOY

As I reflected on the models of courage I interviewed for this book, including the seven courage pilgrims I have introduced you to, I noticed a striking theme in my research and in all our conversations. Despite their different vocations and life experiences, they shared something beyond a demonstration of the seven choices that this book discusses.

From the moment I met each of them, the brightness of their spirit was unmistakable. Not only were all of them optimistic people, but I also discerned that their optimism is inseparable from their courage. Optimism reflects their belief in their purpose, and they live the seven choices as expressions of faith. And because they carry this faith with sincerity, they see ahead of them not only a better world but around them the best in others they interact with. They are not cynical. They engender trust, not suspicion. In conversations with them, they are always present, always listening—accessible, natural, honest—and always giving off a spirit that is positive. Every time I walked away from a conversation with them, I took with me a feeling of hope, confidence, and happiness. And the world responds to them in kind. It meets their optimism with reciprocal support, lowering the cost of risk and making courage easier and sustainable for them.

For each of them, joy is an operating state. It is a bedrock to their optimism and steadies their focus and outlook under pressure. It builds for each of them a trust that enables collaborations and coordinated risk-taking—creating a virtuous cycle of them enabling courage even as they are seeking it.

Joy sustains them as much as it empowers them. Their faith begets courage, in much the same way as their joy begets and amplifies their resilience.

FINAL WORDS—SUSTAIN COURAGE

The road to courage is rarely straight. Systems, structures, and people may restrict your options or try to drain your will. They won't only test your skills; they will test your belief in your own worth. That is why resilience isn't optional—it's the mechanism that keeps courage available over time.

Resilience lets you absorb the hit, recover, and keep choosing your way. It converts setbacks into judgment instead of hesitation. Without it, courage is a spark that extinguishes in the first strong wind. With it, courage becomes a steady capability—repeatable under pressure, durable across cycles.

Courage is not the last item on life's list, reserved for when conditions are perfect. It is a power already within reach. This book exists to remind you that you can exercise it now—and that resilience is what makes that exercise sustainable.

Yes, circumstances matter. Structural headwinds might raise the cost of courageous action, but they do not remove its possibility. If you start from disadvantage, courage becomes an even more essential capacity to build. Your station does not define your agency unless you let it. Resilience keeps that agency intact and serves as that indispensable human freedom that sustains us on the hardest of days.

So I disagreed with my friend in Silicon Valley: courage is not a privilege for the comfortable, and the wrong choice is to let go and give up on the journey. Courage is available to anyone willing to choose it. The tougher the context, the more your return on courage. When the odds feel stacked against you, your courage is the one asset you must not allow anyone to take or trivialize. Invest in it. Build the habits that keep it strong when conditions turn. You may be changed by what happens to you, but resilience ensures you are not reduced by it.

And one more truth from this chapter: joy is not a mood but

a state of being that replenishes resilience—a steadying presence under pressure, restoring optimism and strengthening trust. Choose joy to power resilience; choose resilience to unlock courage.

As we wrap up the journey of this book with concluding thoughts, remember that courage is a must-have for a fulfilling life. Our agency starts the work of finding it, our disciplined choices make it real. In these pages, we named those choices—clarify purpose, own your potential, unmask fear, reject distracting voices, act decisively, grow from failure, and embody resilience (with joy). Together, they form a practical system for a life without regret.

While we are at the end of this book, this is only the start of the rest of your life.

A CALL TO ACTION: EXUDE JOY

Exuding joy is not performance; it's an operating state that strengthens resilience and lowers the cost of courage for you and the people around you. Joy clarifies why the work matters, steadies presence under pressure, and signals trust so others can speak plainly and take smart risks. Practiced daily, joy unlocks not only the best in us, but also the best in others. As a result, it keeps us in the game, healthier, and for the long run.

THE GOAL OF THIS CALL TO ACTION

Make joy a deliberate operating state that replenishes resilience and reduces the personal and social risks of courageous action—expressed through habitual generosity and gratitude.

HOW TO BRING IT TO LIFE

1. **Treat joy as strategic fuel:** It's a resilience multiplier and a trust signal, not a mood.
2. **Model it—visibly:** Practice generosity, gratitude, and emotional steadiness, especially when stakes are high.
3. **Lower the cost of courage:** Use your presence to signal safety; invite candor and smart risk-taking.
4. **Train the muscle:** Build rituals: brief reflections, peer coaching, and intentional prompts before big moments.
5. **Measure what matters:** Track the presence of joy and link it to outcomes (psychological safety, escalation speed, retention, decision quality).
6. **Tell the story:** Share moments when joy made courage possible—especially under pressure.

KEY ENABLERS OR CHALLENGES TO BE MINDFUL OF

- **Life is not always fair:** You have a choice to not dwell too long on what is unfair, but how you can move past it.
- **Safety, not silence:** Don't use "joy" to deflect concerns—protect truth-telling. Practice how to engage constructively.
- **Be generous and grateful:** Share your gifts and recognize the gifts of others.
- **Boundaries create capacity:** Protect sleep, movement, and thinking time; cap after-hours pings. Joy is not overwork—burnout erodes resilience.

Close this book; put joy to work. Practice tangible generosity—do the helpful thing before you're asked. If you feel appreciation, express it. Joy multiplies when it's specific and shared. Make it easier for someone to be courageous because you chose to be generous today.

Onward—with thanks on your tongue, open hands, and goodwill.

CONCLUSION

"I know why the caged bird sings!"

—PAUL LAURENCE DUNBAR

In the region of Galicia in northwestern Spain, thirty miles from the Atlantic Ocean, sits the city of Santiago de Compostela. Legend has it that after his execution, the body of James, one of Jesus' disciples, was transported by the faithful and placed in a tomb in the city center, and a mighty basilica was built over it. Since the ninth century, pilgrims from around Europe have been traveling along a network of routes that lead to the shrine of the apostle, located underneath the splendidly ornate altar of the Cathedral of Santiago de Compostela. Today, the Camino de Santiago, also known as the Way of St. James, is one of the "three great pilgrimages of Christendom."[83]

In 2024 alone, five hundred thousand pilgrims arrived in the large square in front of the majestic cathedral. I was among them.

My Camino began at the base of the Pyrenees in France. I did not know then what those three weeks that started in the medieval town of Saint-Jean-Pied-de-Port would mean to me. What I found was not simply a long walk across Spain—but a mirror of life itself.

The Camino began the way every pilgrimage and courageous act begins—with a single step. It is deceptively simple, yet that first step is everything. What follows is a road of uneven terrain, unpredictable weather, aching feet, and moments of doubt. And yet, alongside the hardship come companionship, resilience, and fulfillment.

Every day, strangers became family. Stories were exchanged in the language of hope, loss, faith, and renewal. Each pilgrim was driven by a purpose—different in detail but united in spirit. By the time I arrived at the Cathedral of Santiago de Compostela, I knew the Camino was not just a pilgrimage. It was a profound lesson in how courage works.

Like life, the Camino taught me that no one can walk your path for you. No two routes are identical, but for all the pilgrims, the call was the same: *to keep walking, to keep choosing, to keep becoming.*

THE WAY OF COURAGE

The Camino taught me what this book has sought to show: courage is not about a single heroic act but about walking your way, every day, step by step.

Throughout these chapters, we've explored the *seven choices* that lead to courage:

1. **Commit to a Purpose:** Know why you walk.
2. **Own Your Potential:** Believe you are capable of more than you imagine.
3. **Unmask Fear:** Confront the doubts and illusions that hold you back.
4. **Reject Distracting Voices:** Filter the noise to focus on your true calling.

5. **Act Decisively:** Take bold steps, even when the path is unclear.
6. **Grow Through Failure:** Learn from setbacks rather than shrinking from them.
7. **Embody Resilience (and Joy):** Keep walking when the road feels longest and hardest.

These are not theories. They are practices. They have been the steps of many and they have been the steps of my life. They are the steps of your own Camino, not in Spain but in your longer journey to courage. They are how ordinary people become extraordinary in the lives they lead and the impact they make. They don't guarantee anything, but they unlock a lot. As the thinker James Baldwin said, "Not everything that is faced can be changed; but nothing can be changed until it is faced." Face your life with courage.

I wrote this book because I wanted more of us who face lives with regret to change them into celebrations of courage. Courage is not rare, just inconsistently practiced. It is within each of us, waiting to be claimed. It is not about being perfect. It is about presence and persistence.

COURAGE CHOICE ARCHITECTURE

	COURAGEOUS CHOICES		FEARFUL CHOICES	COURAGE IN ACTION
C	Commit to a Purpose	F	Forsake Your Calling	Draft how you want your life remembered
O	Own Your Potential	E	Embody Self-Doubt	Challenge Your Self-Limiting Beliefs
U	Unmask Fear	A	Allow Apprehension to Rule	Make Fear a Decision-Making Prerequisite
R	Reject Distracting Voices	R	React to External Chatter	Set a High Bar for Who Influences You
A	Act Decisively	F	Fail to Follow Through	Master the First Step
G	Grow from Failure	U	Unravel with Setbacks	Seek Progress over Perfection
E	Embody Resilience (and Joy)	L	Let Go and Give Up	Exude Joy

THE JOY OF BECOMING

The evening of our arrival in Santiago de Compostela, I returned after dinner to the large cobble-stoned square in front of the cathedral. I wanted to see, again, and reflect on the powerful monument that had beckoned to so many for centuries and to me for several weeks. The sun was setting, painting the sky in deep shades of orange and violet, its light draped across the stone facades of the magnificent architecture. Other pilgrims—freshened from showers and rest, were drawn back too, and soon there was a large gathering.

On the edge of the square, a small folk band began to play. Slowly, then all at once, a throng of pilgrims circled around them, voices lifted in unison. We sang songs of journey, of struggle, of freedom. The voices were not polished or rehearsed; they were raw, strident, and alive. In that moment, the atmosphere was electric—celebratory and joyful, full of gratitude for the road behind and anticipation for the life ahead. The joy was not passive; it was contagious, pulling each of us into something larger than ourselves—community and anticipation.

Standing there, I realized something that had begun to take shape for me out on the dirt trails of the Camino, and which the truly courageous already know: *the way to courage is through joy.* Giving joy, receiving it back, and letting that cycle of goodwill carry us forward. Courage can feel daunting in isolation, but in the presence of joy, it becomes lighter, more natural, more possible. Joy builds trust. Joy lowers the cost of risk. Joy makes courage easier.

As the music rose and the square filled with song, I knew this was not simply the end of a pilgrimage—it was a beginning. The beginning of living courageously, not as a solitary pursuit but as a shared journey fueled by joy. The beginning of a movement.

SING YOUR SONG LOUDLY

Paul Laurence Dunbar's poem "Sympathy" gave voice to the caged bird, its song born of longing and resilience. It reminds us of a deeper truth: the song within us is not meant to be silenced.

Each of us has a song—a unique purpose and contribution the world needs. Too often, we keep quiet, afraid of judgment, failure, or rejection. But courage demands more. Courage demands that you not only sing your song—but that you sing it loudly so others may hear it and be emboldened to sing theirs.

The world does not need more quiet. It needs voices lifted, strong and clear, creating a chorus of courage that inspires change and possibility.

THE MOVEMENT BEGINS

My Camino taught me that the destination matters, but the journey transforms us. Courage works the same way. It is not a moment—it is a way of living. And like every pilgrimage, it begins with a step.

This is your invitation.

Now is the time to act. Reading is not enough. Reflection is not enough. Courage is only real when lived.

- **Define your purpose** and let it guide your steps.
- **Face your fears** and dismantle them, one by one.
- **Spread courage and joy** wherever you are to build a movement and to sustain you.
- **Sing your song** so the world can hear it and benefit from you.

Courage is not just about you—it is about all of us. When you rise with courage, you give permission for others to rise as well. And when enough of us rise, when we sing together—loudly, joyfully, unapologetically—we transform quiet desperation into a movement of hope and possibility.

You are not destined for desperation or regret. You have a song to sing, embedded in your unique life, which will make a difference in the world that only you can make. No cage or obstacle can stop you if this is your determination. I wish you the best on your journey of courage. I hope that it will be fruitful and that it brings you to a deep and lasting sense of fulfillment and the solace that you gave it your all.

I hope that these words of mine help. I am grateful to have had the opportunity to share them.

Henry David Thoreau spoke of songs left unsung. May yours never be one of them.

THE COURAGE HOUSE

LIVING A LIFE WITHOUT REGRET

Acting intentionally in service of a virtuous core mission or purpose, despite the risks faced in doing so.

C	O	U	R	A	G	E
Commit to a Purpose	Own Your Potential	Unmask Fear	Reject Distracting Voices	Act Decisively	Grow from Failure	Embody Resilience (and Joy)

LIVE FROM THE HEART

IN GRATITUDE

Authoring a book is never a solitary act. It is, in many ways, the culmination of a thousand conversations, countless sacrifices, and the quiet encouragement of those who believed when I hesitated or faltered. This book—about courage, one of the most complicated and necessary human pursuits—could not exist without the many people who lent me their wisdom, time, love, and friendship.

I begin with my parents, Victor and Jael Williams, who opened our eyes to the world and nourished us with a diet of global literature that sowed the seeds for my own byline. To my mother, especially, I am grateful for the many late nights we spent together racing toward essay deadlines for submission to writing competitions. My earliest teachers at Fourah Bay College School in Sierra Leone built the foundation for all my writing. Mrs. E.Z.O. Johnson Oluwole and Mrs. Jestina Jones, chief among many others, offered both instruction and encouragement to a boy who hung on their every word. And to the friends who blazed the trail with their own books and urged me to add mine to the shelves—Soon Yu (*Iconic Advantage, Friction*), Kevin Bethune (*Reimagining Design, Nonlinear*), and Martin Gutmann (*The Unseen Leader*)—thank you for your inspiration.

Many individuals helped broaden my understanding of courage through their scholarship, their practice, and their stories. Among them are friends and family, academic heavyweights, professional coaches, business executives, and military leaders who gave generously of their time and insights. Dr. Emmanuel Nuesiri, whom I first met at African Leadership University (ALU), translated philosophy into vivid, relevant lessons that shaped my thinking. My uncle, Ebenezer Strasser-King, traced courage through our family ancestry with diligence and pride. Branding expert Laura Fravel walked with me through the early, uncertain days of my professional independence, helping me shape courage into something more than a word—a process that evolved into this book project. I am also indebted to Dr. Girish Nuckchady, who had written his PhD dissertation on courage and agreed to sit with me, a stranger to him, over coffee in Port Louis, Mauritius, to discuss it. Professors Thomas DeLong and Scott Snook of Harvard Business School helped me reflect deeply during the short but intense experience of *The Reflective Leader*. Thank you to Jan Rivkin of Harvard Business School, who gave me courage at a time when I sorely needed it. My corporate board accountability family Adimika Arthur, Alicia.R.Schwarz, Rodney Braxton, Lybra Clemons, Audra Cunningham, Ed Magee, Marlene Washington, and Sheraun Britton-Parris with the guidance of Mark D. Goodman, provided testimony that reminded me at a critical time that I was not walking alone. To the many people who granted interviews, short and long, and who shared articles, references, and reflections after learning of my project—your enthusiasm became a mirror of my own, and I thank you. I give special mention to my earliest interviewees, who scaffolded my first thoughts: military veteran Jonathan "JP" Puskas, elite athlete coach Chris Shamrock, Olympian Simidele Adeagbo, and former Nike historian Scott Reames. And to the staff of Harvard Business School's Baker Library—thank you for the invaluable resources.

Some of the stories in this book are also grounded in the lived experiences of courage pilgrims who consented to let me share about their journeys. Ali Hassan Bin Mohd Hassan, for your steadfastness of purpose. Roosevelt Giles, for never being a stranger. Fred Swaniker, for the gift of the ALU experience and for never shying away from hard things. Gary DeStefano, for some of my boldest and most transformational professional experiences. Simidele Adeagbo, for continuing to sleigh and inspire others with your courage against adversity. Wendy Lea, for your openness about pain, resilience, and the dynamo of inspiration you are. The late Janet "Mammy K" King, matriarch of the extended Strasser-King family, who spoke through the many people she shaped in her lifetime about anchoring a life of impact and community leadership in courageous independence.

I also thank the editors who rescued me when I was bogged down: Emily Crookston and Deanna Novak. I am indebted to the beta readers who stress-tested this work—Martin Gutmann, Hope Mutua, Audrey Bracey Deegan, Dr. Memuna Williams, Peter Griffiths, Jim Olson, Emmanuel Nuesiri, Lybra Clemmons, and Dr. Girish Nuckchady. To the development editors—Cathy Fyrock, Emily Crookston, Glynis Charlton, and Adaobi Obi Tulton—your feedback sharpened both language and logic.

This book would not have happened without the dedication and brilliance of the Scribe Media publishing team. Madison Fitzpatrick touched this project more than anyone—your patience, research, and ability to shape my thoughts into better expression were a gift. Teresa Muniz brought courage to life with creativity and art, while Rachael Williams, project manager extraordinaire, and Meg Ahrenberg shepherded the manuscript over sometimes rocky terrain and across the finish line. To the rest of the Scribe Media team, with a special mention of Executive Editor Mark Chait, thank you for your many contributions along the way.

It was humbling to receive early encouragement and praise

for this book from respected and accomplished thought leaders—chief among them Hubert Joly, Kevin Carroll, Fred Swaniker, Paul Polman, Roosevelt Giles, Rinaldo Brutoco, and Deepak Chopra. From the first time I heard it, Helga Hengge's story of mountaineering gave altitude to my words, and I am grateful to her for writing the foreword. Your voices lent courage to mine.

No book finds its audience without partners who help it launch into the world. Thanks to Zach Kristensen, Jenna Owen, and Hannah Cary, and all the well-wishers who joined the launch team—you transformed this book from manuscript into movement. I am also grateful for the TEDx community that helped turn this project into a narrative experience. Martin Gutmann, your TEDx talk was an inspiration. Stefan Balzar and the TEDxBerlin family, thank you for the stage. Niki Skene and Laura Baxter, my TEDx coaches, and Eksteen de Waal—your insights shaped how I told this story aloud.

At critical junctures in my life, individuals extended their hand and opened doors, allowing me to test and refine my courage in many places and spaces the world over. Leroy Keith, former President of Morehouse College, and Sterling Hudson, former Dean of Admissions at Morehouse, made my Morehouse experience possible. Managers, including Chris Harned, Mark Wittman, and David Jeffries (Lehman Brothers), Lynda Sullivan and Mark Lunsford (Gap), Craig Cheek and Gary DeStefano (Nike), Angelo Lagrega (VF Jeanswear), and Roland Auschel (adidas), nurtured me at defining times. I am grateful as well to Fred Swaniker (African Leadership Group) for allowing me to see myself in the faces of two thousand college students, and Richard Arlove, Board Director at African Leadership University, for your counsel and friendship, and to executives who left their imprint on my career—Trevor Edwards, Ron McCray, Gregg James, Gina Warren, Tom Arndorfer, David Heath, Louis Jordan and Gerry Rogers (Nike), and Scott Baxter (Kontoor Brands). Thank you, Kathy Waller, for your continued mentorship on my board governance journey and for the generous example of yours.

Some special individuals I count as my inner circle have already been mentioned, but their influence deserves repeating. Gary DeStefano again, for your lasting imprint on my choices. John and Marcia Brown, for enfolding me into your extended family of mentees. Michael Stanier, whose sincerity and perspective have been a guiding beacon from the evening we first met and had dinner in Erlangen. Juan Pablo Mobili, for your inspirational poetry and for always picking up the phone. And to my lifelong companions in mutual support—Olufemi Anthony, Victor Cole, Leone Elliott, Brian French, Emmanuel Sawyerr, Dabington Taylor, Wanji Williams, Cleminatu Fields, and Alvin Fashu-Kanu—thank you for being constants.

I also traveled longer over the years with many who helped me navigate forks on the road to discovery and courage—the amazing Strasser-King, Williams, Benjamin and George families; the Fourah Bay College School Class of 1983 friendship group; my Morehouse brothers Jamal Miller, Zachary Cross, Zane Hurst, Razab Chowdhury, Kwame Manley, Eric Rice, Michael Toca, Assan Jallow, Garth Forde, Nigel Gomez, and Joseph Massaquoi; Spelman sisters Maya Hamilton and Sharon Barbour; my Lehman Brothers trench warriors of the 1995 Analyst Class, as well as Amini Kajunju and Claranne Jones; Gap Inc. Treasury teammates Lynda Sullivan, Shari Freedman, David Burkart, and Michelle Chan Crouse; Harvard Business School 2002E section-mates, and school mates Aishetu Fatima Dozié, Lisa Bourne, Kola Otitoju, Daniel Ogbonna, Obi Isiadinso, George Osawaye, Chike Obianwu, Ade Lawal, Demola Gbadagesin, and Jean-Philippe Kouakou-Zebouah; Nike colleagues Kathy Hines, Thomas Lwebuga, Kevin Bethune, Paul Nselel, Douffy Youm, Jennifer Yreugas, Clarence Nesbitt, Pamela Neferkara, Gregg James, Omari Leggett, and Amanda Rust; my Malaysia team, who embodied the *boleh* (can do) spirit; fellow Goldman Sachs banking associates Nat Raggette and Craig Vaughan; VF Corporation peers Katherine Cousins, Rich Blaya, and Nancy McClure; and adidas friends and business partners Gregg Tate, Michael Stanier, Guillaume de Monplanet, and María Fernanda Wellner.

There were some who gave me confidence in courage by being key actors in the happy outcomes on the opposite side of fear. Morehouse College made my leap of faith to attend one of the best bets I ever made. My Nike Malaysia team made me glad I made the jump to move across the world. The late Deyinde Robbin Coker hosted my family in The Gambia when they arrived there as refugees from Sierra Leone's civil war. The students, faculty, and staff at ALU welcomed me home and helped me experience what truly fulfilling work feels like. The Trudeau and Camara families helped us make the Netherlands home. Thank you all for showing the life-changing benefits of courage.

The journey of writing this book was also enriched by fellow *peregrinos* I met along the Frances Route of the Camino de Santiago pilgrimage in June 2024—companion seekers, thank you for walking with me. You deepened my understanding of courage in motion.

Finally, I must honor my family, who stood behind me in ways too numerous to capture. To my mother, for creating so many possibilities. To my siblings—Victor, Henderson, and Harriette—for your unwavering belief in me. And to my wife, Debbie, and my children, Maxwell and Vivienne: you gave me the time and space to write and powerful opportunities to discover what courage really means—a debt I cannot repay. This book is as much yours as it is mine.

Every difficulty and triumph in living courage showed up in the process of writing about it. I was able to finish only because of the people named here—and many others unnamed—who embodied the very courage this book seeks to honor. To all of you: thank you.

—CHRISTOPHER O. H. WILLIAMS, NOVEMBER 2025

ABOUT THE AUTHOR

CHRISTOPHER O. H. WILLIAMS is a TEDx speaker and former Fortune 500 executive who serves as a board director, business consultant, executive mentor, and public speaker on strategy, governance, and transformation. His career spans Nike, adidas, VF Corporation, Gap, Goldman Sachs, and Lehman Brothers, where he held management and executive roles shaping enterprise and financial strategy and overseeing market execution. He was the first President of African Leadership University, an institution focused on developing ethical leaders and entrepreneurial managers. As President of Custament Partners, he advises organizations navigating strategic, business-model, and organizational change.

Born in Sierra Leone and a naturalized US citizen, Williams has lived and worked in the United States, Europe, Africa, and Southeast Asia. His functional experience includes strategy, retail, sales, and brand management and work with consumer brands at all stages of life. These diverse contexts—emerging and developed markets, corporate and education, headquarters and field, personal and professional—provide the basis for his reflections on decision-making under pressure covered in his book, *C.O.U.R.A.G.E.* He also speaks to executive audiences internationally and has served in corporate and nonprofit governance roles. Williams is married with two children and divides his time between the United States and the Netherlands.

REFERENCES

1. Matt Powell, "Sneakernomics: June 2014 Sneaker Winners and Losers," *Forbes*, July 16, 2014, https://www.forbes.com/sites/mattpowell/2014/07/16/sneakernomics-june-2014-sneaker-winners-and-losers/.

2. Aaron Ricadela, "Adidas Plunges After Reducing Forecast on Russia, Golf," *Bloomberg*, July 31, 2014, https://www.bloomberg.com/news/articles/2014-07-31/adidas-reduces-2014-profit-forecast-to-miss-2015-targets.

3. Joern Poltz, "Adidas Investor Says Loses Confidence in Management—Report," *Yahoo Finance*, May 3, 2015, https://sg.finance.yahoo.com/news/adidas-investor-says-loses-confidence-management-report-185634758--sector.html.

4. "The adidas Group Presented Its New Strategic 2020 Business Plan 'Creating the New,'" EuropaWire, March 30, 2015, https://news.europawire.eu/the-adidas-group-presented-its-new-strategic-2020-business-plan-creating-the-new-98327699126712/eu-press-release/2015/03/30/22/48/24/33235/.

5. Russell Parsons, "Adidas to Focus Marketing Spend on Six Cities and Ramp up Co-creation," *MarketingWeek*, March 26, 2025, https://www.marketingweek.com/adidas-to-focus-marketing-spend-on-six-cities-and-ramp-up-co-creation/.

6. Bronnie Ware, *The Top Five Regrets of the Dying: A Life Transformed by the Dearly Departing* (Hay House, 2011).

7. Ware, *The Top Five Regrets of the Dying*.

8. *Ibid.*

9   Sissela Bok, *Exploring Happiness: From Aristotle to Brain Science* (Yale University Press, 2010).

10 *Merriam-Webster Dictionary*, s.v. "courage," https://www.merriam-webster.com/dictionary/courage.

11 "The Highest Good: An Introduction to the 4 Stoic Virtues," Daily Stoic, lasted modified August 31, 2020, https://dailystoic.com/4-stoic-virtues/.

12 Darrell Dobbs, "For Lack of Wisdom: Courage and Inquiry in Plato's 'Laches'," *The Journal of Politics* 48, no. 4 (1986): 825–849, https://www.jstor.org/stable/2131002.

13 Richard Kraut, "Aristotle's Ethics," *The Stanford Encyclopedia of Philosophy*, ed. Edward N. Zalta and Uri Nodelman, revised July 2, 2022, https://plato.stanford.edu/entries/aristotle-ethics/.

14 Kraut, "Aristotle's Ethics."

15 Dale Wilkerson, "Friedrich Nietzsche," *Internet Encyclopedia of Philosophy,* https://iep.utm.edu/nietzsch/.

16 "Our Cultural Home," Voortrekker Monument, https://vtm.org.za/en/cultural-home/.

17 Joseph Epstein, "The Four-Way Test in a Post-Truth Era," *Rotary*, https://www.rotary.org/en/four-way-test-post-truth-era.

18 Ulrich Janse van Vuuren, "67 Things Nelson Mandela Said That Made the World a Better Place," *One*, July 18, 2015, https://www.one.org/africa/stories/67-things-nelson-mandela-said-that-made-the-world-a-better-place/.

19 Aristotle, *Nicomachean Ethics* (Loeb Classical Library, 1926), 165, https://www.loebclassics.com/view/aristotle-nicomachean_ethics/1926/pb_LCL073.165.xml?readMode=recto.

20 University of Exeter, "Herd Mentality: Are We Programmed to Make Bad Decisions?" *ScienceDaily*, December 16, 2014, www.sciencedaily.com/releases/2014/12/141216212049.htm.

21 "Top 10 CEO Scandals," *TIME*, https://content.time.com/time/specials/packages/completelist/0,29569,2009445,00.html.

22 John Bunyan, *The Pilgrim's Progress: From This World to That Which Is to Come* (S.I. Bell, 1891).

23 Naina Dhingra and Bill Schaninger, "The Search for Purpose at Work," McKinsey & Company, accessed October 8, 2025, https://www.mckinsey.com/capabilities/people-and-organizational-performance/our-insights/the-search-for-purpose-at-work.

24 As quoted by her biographer Sarah Hopkins Bradford in 1869.

25 The origin of this quote is unclear, and it has been attributed to several individuals including Irene Dunne, Peter Marshall, and Malcolm X.

26 This quote appeared in a speech delivered in Accra, Ghana, on July 10, 1953.

27 Patrick H. Breen, "Nat Turner's Revolt (1831)," *Encyclopedia Virginia*, December 7, 2020, accessed October 1, 2025, https://encyclopediavirginia.org/entries/turners-revolt-nat-1831/.

28 "Sierra Leonean Heroes," Sierra Leone Web, accessed October 1, 2025, https://www.sierra-leone.org/Heroes/heroes5.html.

29 Jim Afremow, *The Champion's Mind: How Great Athletes Think, Train, and Thrive* (Rodale Books, 2014).

30 Sahithya Senthil Kumaran, "Charles Schulz | The Success Story of the Peanuts Comic Strip Creator," *Failure Before Success*, August 25, 2021, accessed October 1, 2025, https://failurebeforesuccess.com/charles-schulz-the-success-story-of-the-peanuts-comic-strip-creator/.

31 "J.K. Rowling's Story of Rejection Before Harry Potter's Success," *Inspire and Rise*, accessed October 1, 2025, https://www.inspireandrise.com/jk-rowlings-journey-before-harry-potter-success/.

32 Pratap Solution, "The Hidden Struggles That Shaped Oprah Winfrey's Career Beginnings," *Pratap Solution*, June 14, 2024, accessed October 1, 2025, https://www.pratapsolution.com/2024/06/the-hidden-struggles-that-shaped-oprah.html?m=1.

33 Barack Obama, *The Audacity of Hope: Thoughts on Reclaiming the American Dream* (Penguin Random House, 2007).

34 This quote is widely attributed to Carl Lewis, though it's difficult to pinpoint a specific event or interview where he might have said it (https://www.goodreads.com/author/quotes/780047.Carl_Lewis).

35 "Wangari Maathai—Facts," *NobelPrize.org*, accessed October 1, 2025, https://www.nobelprize.org/prizes/peace/2004/maathai/facts/.

36 Kate Kershner and Austin Henderson, "What's the Baader-Meinhof Phenomenon?," *HowStuffWorks*, September 5, 2023, accessed October 1, 2025, https://science.howstuffworks.com/life/inside-the-mind/human-brain/baader-meinhof-phenomenon.htm.

37 "How Self-Talk in Sports Performance Boosts Focus and Motivation," *Athletic Insight*, February 12, 2025, accessed October 1, 2025, https://www.athleticinsight.com/sports-psychology/self-talk.

38 https://www.helgahengge.com/

39 Howard E. LeWine, MD (reviewer), "Understanding the Stress Response," *Harvard Health Publishing*, July 6, 2020, https://www.health.harvard.edu/staying-healthy/understanding-the-stress-response.

40 Kenneth Araullo, "Global Premium Trends Reflect Evolving Risk and Protection Needs—Allianz," *Insurance Business*, May 27, 2025, https://www.insurancebusinessmag.com/us/news/breaking-news/global-premium-trends-reflect-evolving-risk-and-protection-needs--allianz-536992.aspx.

41 "Recent Executive Actions on Diversity, Equity, and Inclusion (DEI)," *Congressional Research Service*, January 29, 2025, accessed October 1, 2025, https://www.congress.gov/crs-product/IN12497.

42 Andre M. Perry et al., "Black Wealth Is Increasing, But So Is the Racial Wealth Gap." *The Brookings Institute*, January 9, 2024, https://www.brookings.edu/articles/black-wealth-is-increasing-but-so-is-the-racial-wealth-gap/#:~:text=According%20to%20the%20latest%20data%20from%20the,white%20household%20and%20the%20median%20Black%20household.

43 "Racial and Ethnic Inequality Has Cost U.S. Economy $51 Trillion Since 1990," *The World Economic Forum*, September 12, 2021, https://www.weforum.org/stories/2021/09/racial-and-ethnic-inequality-has-cost-us-economy-51-trillion-since-1990/.

44 Kelsey Garrett, "How Mauritius Handled COVID-19 and What the United States Could Learn From the Tiny Island Nation," *Pulitzer Center*, accessed October 1, 2025, https://pulitzercenter.org/stories/how-mauritius-handled-covid-19-and-what-united-states-could-learn-tiny-island-nation.

45 Neil Edwards, "Rwanda's Successes and Challenges in Response to COVID-19," *Atlantic Council*, March 24, 2020, accessed October 1, 2025, https://www.atlanticcouncil.org/blogs/africasource/rwandas-successes-and-challenges-in-response-to-covid-19/; Fred Swaniker (@@FredSwaniker), X (formerly Twitter), November 15, 2023, accessed October 1, 2025, https://x.com/FredSwaniker/status/1724682799918018989.

46 Carol S. Dweck, *Mindset: The New Psychology of Success*, updated ed. (Ballantine Books, 2016).

47 As composed in 1873 by Philip Paul Bliss.

48 https://www.edelman.com/trust/2024/trust-barometer

49 University of Exeter, "Herd Mentality."

50 Originally from Johann Hari, a journalist and author. In his book, *Chasing the Scream: The First and Last Days of the War on Drugs*, he writes: "The opposite of addiction is not sobriety. It is human connection."

51 "Where the Heart Is: The Krio of Sierra Leone," *YAME*, March 11, 2019, accessed October 1, 2025, https://yame.space/culturelinks/2019/3/11/where-the-heart-is-the-krio-of-sierra-leone.

52 Joshua J. Mark, "1521 Excommunication of Luther: Complete Text," *World History Encyclopedia*, December 15, 2021, accessed October 1, 2025, https://www.worldhistory.org/article/1903/1521-excommunication-of-luther-complete-text/.

53 "Galileo Goes on Trial for Heresy," *History*, accessed October 1, 2025, https://www.history.com/this-day-in-history/april-12/galileo-is-accused-of-heresy.

54 Gillian Brockell, "Rep. Barbara Lee Voted Against War in Afghanistan. She Was Mocked for It," *Washington Post*, August 17, 2021, https://www.washingtonpost.com/history/2021/08/17/barbara-lee-afghanistan-vote/.

55 https://www.edelman.com/trust/2024/trust-barometer

56 Kim Scott, *Radical Candor: Be a Kick-Ass Boss Without Losing Your Humanity* (St. Martin's Press, 2017).

57 "Mar. 7, 1965 | AL Law Enforcement Attacks Civil Rights Activists on 'Bloody Sunday' in Selma," *Equal Justice Initiative*, accessed October 1, 2025, https://calendar.eji.org/racial-injustice/mar/7.

58 Originally published six years after Bonhoeffer's death in 1945, the book was made up of materials gathered and selected by his friend Eberhard Bethge.

59 Amy Tikkanen, "US Airways Flight 1549," *Britannica*, last updated August 29, 2025, https://www.britannica.com/topic/US-Airways-Flight-1549-incident.

60 Marcia Blenko, Eric Garton, Ludovica Mottura, and Oliver Wright, "Winning Operating Models That Convert Strategy to Results," *Bain & Company*, December 10, 2014, accessed October 1, 2025, https://www.bain.com/insights/winning-operating-models-that-convert-strategy-to-results/.

61 "NIKE, Inc. 2013 Investor Day Transcript—Complete with Q&A," Nike, Inc., October 9, 2013, accessed October 1, 2025, https://s1.q4cdn.com/806093406/files/doc_events/NIKE,%20Inc.%202013%20Investor%20Day%20Transcript%20-%20Complete%20with%20QA%20-%20FINAL.pdf. This transcript is provided by NIKE, Inc. only for reference purposes. Information presented was current only as of October 9, 2013, and may have subsequently changed materially. NIKE, Inc. does not update or delete outdated information contained in this transcript, and disclaims any obligation to do so.

62 Derek Sivers, "First Follower: Leadership Lessons from Dancing Guy," YouTube, February 11, 2010, https://www.youtube.com/watch?v=fW8amMCVAJQ.

63 "Investor News Details," Nike, June 29, 2023, https://investors.nike.com/investors/news-events-and-reports/investor-news/investor-news-details/2023/NIKE-Inc.-Reports-Fiscal-2023-Fourth-Quarter-and-Full-Year-Results/default.aspx.

64 "Martin Niemöller: 'First They Came For...,'" Holocaust Encyclopedia, lasted edited April 11, 2023, https://encyclopedia.ushmm.org/content/en/article/martin-niemoeller-first-they-came-for-the-socialists.

65 "President Kagame of Rwanda Calls Out Global Apathy That Caused 1994 Genocide," *The Hindu*, April 8, 2024, accessed October 1, 2025, https://www.thehindu.com/news/international/president-kagame-of-rwanda-calls-out-global-apathy-that-caused-1994-genocide/article68041822.ece.

66 Chunka Mui, "How Kodak Failed," *Forbes*, January 18, 2012, https://www.forbes.com/sites/chunkamui/2012/01/18/how-kodak-failed/.

67 Travis Sharrow, "The Rise and Fall of Giants: What Happened to Kodak and Nokia?," *SoftHandTech*, accessed October 1, 2025, https://softhandtech.com/what-happened-to-kodak-and-nokia/.

68 Mike Isaac, "Inside Uber's Aggressive, Unrestrained Workplace Culture," *New York Times*, February 22, 2017, https://www.nytimes.com/2017/02/22/technology/uber-workplace-culture.html.

69 Bill George, "Why Boeing's Problems with the 737 MAX Began More Than 25 Years Ago," *Working Knowledge*, Harvard Business School, accessed October 1, 2025, https://www.library.hbs.edu/working-knowledge/why-boeings-problems-with-737-max-began-more-than-25-years-ago.

70 Jeff Horwitz, "The Facebook Files," *Wall Street Journal*, September 2021, https://www.wsj.com/articles/the-facebook-files-11631713039.

71 American Psychological Association, "What Is Exposure Therapy?," accessed October 8, 2025, https://www.apa.org/ptsd-guideline/patients-and-families/exposure-therapy.

72 "How Princess Diana Changed Attitudes to Aids," BBC News, April 5, 2017, https://www.bbc.com/news/av/magazine-39490507.

73 "Space Shuttle Columbia," Wikipedia, last updated May 5, 2025, https://en.wikipedia.org/wiki/Space_Shuttle_Columbia.

74 Elizabeth Howell, "Columbia Disaster: What Happened, What NASA Learned," Space.com, accessed October 1, 2025, https://www.space.com/19436-columbia-disaster.html.

75 Spark, "The Unfortunate Chain of Events That Led to the Columbia Disaster," YouTube video, June 8, 2025, https://youtu.be/VdezNT7TgIo.

76 Gabriella Frisch, "PR Time Machine: The Netflix Price Hike Debacle," Prosek Partners (blog), January 9, 2025, https://www.prosek.com/unboxed-thoughts/pr-time-machine-the-netflix-price-hike-debacle/.

77 Bruce McCall, "The Horror of Rejection," *New Yorker*, October 12, 1998, https://www.newyorker.com/magazine/1998/10/12/the-horror-of-rejection.

78 "Simidele Adeagbo," Wikipedia, last updated September 6, 2025, https://en.wikipedia.org/wiki/Simidele_Adeagbo.

79 Barney Salzberg, *Beautiful Oops!* (Hachette Book Group, 2010).

80 Dina Gerdeman, "Minorities Who 'Whiten' Job Resumes Get More Interviews," *Harvard Business School*, May 17, 2017, https://www.library.hbs.edu/working-knowledge/minorities-who-whiten-job-resumes-get-more-interviews.

81 Cooper Allen, "Justice Ketanji Brown Jackson Reflects on Her Historic Journey," University of Virginia School of Law, September 18, 2025, https://www.law.virginia.edu/news/202509/justice-ketanji-brown-jackson-reflects-her-historic-journey.

82 Christina Cerrega and Chauncey Alcorn, "'Nobody's Going to Steal That Joy': Cory Booker's Full Speech to Katanji Brown Jackson, Annotated," *Capital B*, March 25, 2022, https://capitalbnews.org/booker-ketanji-brown-jackson-full-speech/#:~:text=The%20way%20you%20have%20dealt,actually%20out%20of%20the%20norm.

83 History Committee, "History: El Camino De Santiago," Saint James' Episcopal Church, Warrenton, VA, April 13, 2016, https://www.saintjameswarrenton.org/news/history-el-camino-de-santiago.

www.ingramcontent.com/pod-product-compliance
Lightning Source LLC
Chambersburg PA
CBHW060518080526
44586CB00012B/526